How's Your Computer-Side Manner?

ADVANCE PRAISE FOR
HOW'S YOUR COMPUTER-SIDE MANNER?

As a CEO and inclusion catalyst, I know all too well how important effective communication skills are. *How's Your Computer-Side Manner?* is one of the most valuable communication skills books I've seen. It is filled with engaging examples and practical tactics for being a better communicator. I highly recommend Ali's book to *any* leader who wants to take their communication skills to the next level!

~Amy Waninger, CEO, Lead At Any Level

We were all taught that communication is a two-way street. I would argue it's more like a three-lane roundabout. Ali's book, *How's Your Computer Side Manner?*, is like a calm passenger guiding you through it.

~Jason Carney, vice president,
Human Resources for Rehab Medical

How's Your Computer-Side Manner? is an eye-opening reminder that *every* communication counts. A must-read for any leader.

~Eliese Davis, manager, Talent Development,
Indiana Farm Bureau Insurance

Computer-side manner is a twenty-first-century concept worth mastering. Ali Atkison, Ph.D., makes the brilliant case that we cannot afford to use online messaging conventions as an excuse for poor communication skills. When creating an impression of you, there is no separating digital and in-person communications and interactions in the judgments of the people who receive and react to our communications. Dr. Atkison offers practical advice to help you avoid the most common communication mistakes and dispels many myths. *How's Your Computers-Side Manner?* will help you stop being a digital polluter and keep you from poisoning your reputation.

~**Andy Dix,** MS, BCC

As a communications professional, I know the importance of clear, concise, and impactful communication for accomplishing our business objectives. Dr. Ali's book should be *the* go-to hand-book for any professional who wants to ensure their communication goals—personal or professional—are always accomplished.

~**Laura McCaffrey,** vice president of Public Affairs and Communications, Indiana Hospital Association

When I first heard Ali Atkison use the phrase "computer-side manner" I was struck by how on-point she was. As someone who communicates a lot through digital methods, I needed to learn more! As I read *How's Your Computer-Side Manner?,* I laughed at how many of these faux pas I have been guilty of over the years. *How's Your Computer-Side Manner?* is a must-read for anyone who communicates through email, video, text, or chat!

~**Jeffrey S. Ton,** author, *Amplify Your Value*

Living in an age of information, and an abundance of information that is not all equal value, means it is easy to overlook the importance of how information is shared. *How's Your Computer-Side Manner? The 9 Digital Communication Mistakes You're Making That Are Holding You Back* is a great aid and reminder that caring for the recipient of our information can be just as important as the information you wish to share. This is a must-read for anyone who has responsibility to sharing accurate and important information.

~**Jason Clifford,** assistant vice present,
Product Development, dormakaba

The best part of Ali's book is that the chapters are structured to dive in where you want to learn and grow. While Ali provides great research for these concepts, she backs up the science with relatable stories to make the application of the research stick. You can read the book all the way through or skip around to focus on specific areas to improve. A great resource to go back to time and again.

~**Gretchen Schott,** chief learning officer, Threefold

How's Your Computer-side Manner? is a testament to the criticality of getting communication right, both personally and professionally. Dr. Ali Atkison brings to light the critical impacts of our lackluster communication skills. The good news is, we can fix them—and Ali shares great insights and tips for improvement! Everyone should read this!

~**Jennifer Cummings,** director, Talent Programs, Sodexo

As someone who is too casual in my digital communication and rarely interacts in person with the people I'm communicating with, I found *How's Your Computer-Side Manner?* super helpful and have already started making changes to my emails and IMs. Ali's book is a must-read for everyone who communicates digitally: in-office personnel, exclusively WHF, recent grads, and seasoned executives. Digital communication is a vital skill nowadays, and Dr. Ali puts it in ways we can comprehend and put into practice immediately. I've applied her practices and have found my colleagues and coworkers are responding more positively to me. 10/10!

~**Megan Clawson,** director of Sales and Marketing, DUZcart

How's Your Computer-Side Manner? is an empowering and incredibly relevant read . . . from the very first page, it was like I was holding up a mirror, reflecting on how I show up and communicate in all of my interactions. Across the nine digital communication techniques that Dr. Atkison highlights, there are practical takeaways that I can implement immediately to improve my communication, and as Dr. Atkison pointed out, improve my brand. *How's Your Computer-Side Manner?* is for anyone wanting to enhance their influence and strengthen their communication, not only online, but in all aspects of their life.

~**Andrea Butcher,** CEO at HRD and author of *The Power in the Pivot* and *HR Kit for Dummies*

The timing for *How's Your Computer-Side Manner?* could not be more perfect. The massive shift to remote work has brought with it new challenges that most people aren't equipped for—let *How's Your Computer-Side Manner?* be your guide.

~**Dan Abeln,** VP of Marketing Analytics and Data Science

Dr. Atkison has written a clear, concise, and compelling book on communication skills that stands out to me for its humor and practical tips, but most of all, for its serious value as a resource for building communication skills that will help you get ahead, whatever your professional goals.

~**Art Pizzello,** principal,
HRD-A Leadership Development Company

Effective communication is what moves business forward. Ali Atkison does a masterful job in calling out the landmines that are present in our "computer-side" communication styles. This is an important read for anyone who is part of a team, leads a team or interacts with others outside of their organization.

~**Scott Nicholson,** partner,
HRD-A Leadership Development Company

In this insightful book, Dr. Ali Atkison skillfully navigates the complexities of human interaction in the virtual world, offering invaluable guidance on fostering empathy, clear communication, and respect in our online interactions. A must-read for anyone seeking to thrive in the age of screens and keyboards.

~**Erica Terkhorn,** VP of Business Operations,
HRD-A Leadership Development Company

In our fast-paced world where well-written communications and face-to-face interactions are often replaced by emails, texts, IMs, online chats and Zoom meetings, Doctor Ali Atkison reminds us that while communication mechanisms may have changed, the importance of clear communications remains. *How's Your Computer-side Manner? The 9 Digital Communication Mistakes You're Making That Are Holding You Back* offers great practical advice on how to ensure your digital communications are effective.

~**MaryBeth Costello,** VP Human Resources, Encore Global

In my line of work, compelling communication skills are critical. Without them, we cannot effectively advocate for our cause or build the collaborative relationships needed to accomplish our mission. Words are the tools we use to enlighten, inspire and empower action. Dr. Atkison has written a book that will prove essential in strengthening the readers' communication skills and provides tips delivered with a touch of humor for an engaging read. I encourage all leaders to read *How's Your Computer-Side Manner?*—and share it with their colleagues.

~**John Robert Smith,** chairman, Transportation for America

Who thought reading about mistakes would be so fun? Dr. Ali's approach of storytelling and research draw us in to help us understand the mistakes we are making and how to overcome them . . . *How's Your Computer-Side Manner?* is timely and insightful and *oh so* relevant to not just professionals, but to all people.

~**Amanda Areces,** vice president of Client Experience, HRD-A Leadership Development Company

I believe in the power of communication to accomplish great things, but also to diminish relationships and reputation if not done well. *How's Your Computer-Side Manner?* shows us how we may be unaware of some of the communication mistakes we're making—and the impact they're having on our professional reputation and our relationships. It is a refreshing take on a longstanding important topic, and I'm so glad I read it. You should, too!

~**Becky Traweek,** CEO, Girl Scouts of Greater Mississippi

This is the book I wish I read prior to the pandemic. The lessons in *How's Your Computer-Side Manner?* are incredibly important to anyone with the desire to be influential in today's business world.

~**Eric Jung,** president, CEO,
Northeastern REMC Power Cooperative

When you change your conversation, you change your results. Words matter when it comes to realizing results. Dr. Ali's book is THE go-to-guide for anyone wanting to build your brand as a trustworthy professional.

~**Karen Mangia,** *WSJ* best-selling author,
executive coach, & tech executive

Insightful. Compelling. Timely. *How's Your Computer-Side Manner?* is the essential guide for effective communication in the future of work.

~**Jason Cochran,** organizational psychologist,
Humanworks8, and co-host of the Geeks, Geezers,
and Googlization podcast

How's Your Computer-Side Manner? offers relatable real-life examples to illustrate mistakes we all make, and it includes practical and straightforward solutions we can apply right away.

~**Lauri Osborne,** director, Talent Management

How's Your Computer-Side Manner? kicks off brilliantly with Chapter 2, Mistake #1: Thinking Your Industry Knowledge is the Only Thing That Matters. Being a leader of IT in a corporation with a WFH model, this content speaks volumes!

~**Jennifer Kier,** director of IT

How's Your Computer-side Manner? The 9 Digital Communication Mistakes You're Making That Are Holding You Back is a unique and timely story. In this digital age, communication, more importantly, healthy communication is crucial for inspiring those around us. *How's Your Computer-Side Manner?* is a collection of advice applicable to your professional and personal life for success in building and maintaining relationships. As a coach, I am consistently working with my clients to remind them, there is no substitute for exceptional communication and connection.

~**Brooke Crosley,** president, Crosley, Inc.

I really like the "computer-side manner" concept. *How's Your Computer-Side Manner?* offers practical, easy-to-implement solutions to avoid common communication mistakes. Everyone can take advantage of these ideas to improve their communications and their team's productivity.

~**Rich Cherry,** chief information officer, SafeBuilt

With a long overdue examination of communication best practices in the digital twenty-first century, Dr. Ali Atkison provides us with practical and powerful tools for success in any field. Reading *How's Your Computer-Side Manner?* encouraged me to not only reflect on my own "computer-side manner" but also take clear and intentional steps to improve my communication skills at every level. Rooted in her own considerable experience, Dr. Atkison supplements her highly relevant anecdotes with serious research, making for an entertaining but yet substantive read. She effectively makes the case that improving our digital communication habits will improve not only our professional prospects, but also the information ecosystem in which we all swim. Bravo!

~Anthony Molinaro, Carnegie Mellon University

Ali Atkison's *How's Your Computer-Side Manner?* is the Rosetta Stone of human communication in a digital world. She navigates and offers solutions to the nine pitfalls of screen-to-screen chat brilliantly. Don't get left behind. Read Ali's book.

~Ira S. Wolfe, Future of Work Global Thought Leader, Entrepreneur, Podcaster, Author

HOW'S YOUR
COMPUTER-SIDE
MANNER?

THE 9 DIGITAL COMMUNICATION
MISTAKES YOU'RE MAKING THAT ARE
HOLDING YOU BACK

Dr. Ali Atkison

NEW YORK

LONDON • NASHVILLE • MELBOURNE • VANCOUVER

How's Your Computer-Side Manner?

The 9 Digital Communication Mistakes You're Making That Are Holding You Back

Published in New York, New York, by Morgan James Publishing. Morgan James is a trademark of Morgan James, LLC. www.MorganJamesPublishing.com

Proudly distributed by Publishers Group West®

Morgan James BOGO™

A **FREE** ebook edition is available for you or a friend with the purchase of this print book.

CLEARLY SIGN YOUR NAME ABOVE

Instructions to claim your free ebook edition:
1. Visit MorganJamesBOGO.com
2. Sign your name CLEARLY in the space above
3. Complete the form and submit a photo of this entire page
4. You or your friend can download the ebook to your preferred device

ISBN 9781636983066 paperback
ISBN 9781636983073 ebook
Library of Congress Control Number: 2023944540

Cover & Interior Design by:
Christopher Kirk
www.GFSstudio.com

Morgan James is a proud partner of Habitat for Humanity Peninsula and Greater Williamsburg. Partners in building since 2006.

Get involved today! Visit: www.morgan-james-publishing.com/giving-back

*To my husband, Adam, for his immutable support of me,
his love of life, his unending positivity, and for teaching me
that everything is figureoutable.*

*To Momma. The apple didn't fall very far, did it?
And I'm so incredibly grateful for it.*

I love you both with everything I have.

TABLE OF CONTENTS

Thinking Your Industry Knowledge Is the Only Thing That Matters

Thinking That the Onus Is on the Other Person to Figure Out What You Mean when Your Communication Is Unclear or Poorly Written

Thinking IM Communication Doesn't Count

ACKNOWLEDGMENTS

I would like to thank my editor, who happens to be my mother, for her collaboration (on this book and in life).

Big thanks to my coach, Jenni Robbins, without whom I would not have endeavored to write this book.

Thank you to my publisher, Morgan James, for the support and guidance.

I want to thank Gabrielle Hendryx-Parker, who gave me the idea for the concept of computer-side manner.

And I owe a huge debt of gratitude to all the leaders who lent their thoughts about the impact of communication skills on their organizations to this book: Gretchen Schott, Gabrielle Hendryx-Parker, Emily Brager, Jason Clifford, Becky Traweek, Greg Norton, and MaryBeth Costello. Thank you all!

FOREWORD

I n the years ahead, you'll be doing more of your work digitally, virtually, and online, not less. We're increasingly forced to sell and serve from a distance—and to connect and communicate across a divide. The digital environments in which we're operating more often are at odds with millennia of face-to-face human evolution; our ability to make safe, confident choices online is challenged.

With this trend comes the continued proliferation of digital noise and digital pollution. They've both been problematic for years. The rise of automated and artificially intelligent systems exacerbates the issue, as bot-driven messages, posts, and content overwhelms us and drowns out what's actually written, created, and sent by authentic human beings.

We regard digital noise as relatively benign; it's the sheer volume of demands on your attention that await us in your inbox, text messages, social feeds, and all the other channels. Digital pollution, however, is the subset of that noise that's especially unwelcome and distracting. The growth of both noise and pollution is exponential.

At its most extreme, digital pollution is intentionally created by the source to harm the recipient. From the source: spam, malware, cyber-attacks, phishing schemes, spoofed email addresses, stolen social profiles, data breaches, and similar. For the recipient: Is this link safe to click? Is this attachment safe to download? Is this from who it says it's from? It's hard enough to sift through all of the noise, but we also have to stay on alert and protect ourselves from the pollution. The level of distrust inherent in digital environments is inflamed. And our vulnerabilities are exploited.

Though the psychological and behavioral impacts of intentional pollution are dramatic, innocent and consequential digital pollution take their toll, too. And each of us creates both. Innocent pollution is created with no ill-intent, but with some ignorance or laziness. It's that "reply all" response that wasn't necessary or the group message that would have been better sent one to one. With a more selfish motivation, consequential pollution inconveniences or interrupts recipients to help the source get what they want. This communication fails to meet recipients halfway or to consider their needs. Negative impact wasn't the goal, but it was a reasonably anticipated outcome that was tolerated by the source.

Is this message or post pollution? What was the intent? You, as the source, don't get to decide. Your recipient does. And they're making these judgments amid a sea of noise and pollution in a digital environment that obscures the details they need to make safe and confident choices. At risk are your relationships, your reputation, and your revenue.

Over millennia, we've evolved to judge not just what people are saying, but how they're saying it. This is a defense and survival mechanism; it's innate and universal across humans. But our faceless, typed-out text in digital spaces lacks the visual and emotional content that our recipients are naturally, automatically, and instinctually seeking. To overcome this challenge and to find success demands a little more thought and care than most of us are bringing to each message and moment.

We're too deep into the digital shift to feign ignorance of this. And the consequences are too significant not to clean up your act. There's a better way—one that puts others' needs and interests on a level playing field with your own, one that's for and about others, and one that results in greater success. And Dr. Ali Atkison shows it to you in these pages.

For decades, Ali 's been dedicated to understanding how the adult brain learns and improving human communication—in both academic settings and in the business world. Though we came to research, explore, and publish on these themes and topics from the perspective of sales and marketing communication, we felt with Ali an immediate and obvious kinship. We also share a fundamental goal: to help people communicate and connect more effectively, even when restricted to digital channels.

The three of us care about communication because we care about relationships. And we know you do, too. Think about it in Ali's words: "If everyone in this world was a better communicator, this world would be a better place." It's as simple, profound, and promising as that.

For better or worse, digital communication is an increasingly important part of *human* communication. Despite the decades that this has been true, we remain, on average, ill-equipped, ill-adapted, and underperforming. As Ali makes clear in these pages: this is a choice. And we can make a better one. We owe it to ourselves and to each other to be more clear, empathetic, and intentional in the way we approach and execute our calls, messages, and meetings. We just need some motivation and some insight. And it's all here.

-Ethan Beute and Stephen Pacinelli,
Wall Street Journal bestselling co-authors
of *Human-Centered Communication*
and *Rehumanize Your Business*

INTRODUCTION

'I've been studying communication since I was an under-graduate majoring in communication at Northern Illinois University, then at Indiana University-Purdue University at Indianapolis (IUPUI). I continued my journey to learn about communication by earning my Ph.D. in Human Communication Studies from the University of Denver.

I've spent my entire adult career researching, teaching, facilitating, writing, and speaking about communication skills. Because of what I do for a living, people often assume that I never make communication mistakes or errors in judgment in my written communication, and that I have perfectly conflict-free relationships. Of course, that can't really be true. I am human, after all.

I've led with emotion and said the wrong thing (in writing and in person) many times. I've made many mistakes, some of which I'm humbled by, and some I outright regret. All of them I hope never to repeat.

In writing this book, I am certainly not presenting myself as a perfect communicator. And I am not suggesting that you should be one either. The point of this book is never to shame anyone for mistakes made, but rather to highlight why we tend to make those mistakes and to offer tools and strategies for making better choices.

I think one of the most important things a person can have is a growth mindset, and by reading this book you're already demonstrating that you have one! Let's tap into our growth mindset as I share the two main tenets of this book:

1. Communication is a choice. We choose our words, and no one is responsible for that choice but us.
2. The words we choose should always be informed by the impact on the other person.

This realization that communication is a choice is critical. And we get to make that choice over and over, hundreds of times a day. **What a gift it is when we realize the choice is ours to make!** We are not victims of our communication style. We are the masters of that destiny.

This book offers you tools to more easily make communication choices that build strong relationships—personal and professional. Although this is not technically a book on brain-based communication (though I do facilitate that particular topic in my work), I do, where relevant, explain the science that supports my assertions and strategies.

Although this book is quite practical in its approach, I have tried to imbue it with humor, as I find levity to be a powerful tool for opening us up for self-reflection and growth. It is my belief that the world would be a more beautiful place if we all communicated more intently with others in mind. Thank you for joining me in this journey to beautify the world through communication!

Chapter 1

ARE YOU A DIGITAL POLLUTER?

Do you ever feel completely inundated by electronic communication? Most of us do nowadays, and it's no wonder. The average professional receives 120 emails a day and sends forty. The average adult under forty-five sends and receives more than eight-five texts per day. It's difficult to find current statistics on how many instant messages are sent each day, but just imagine how many you send and receive, and I bet it's a lot! And, if you can believe this, the average American is exposed to anywhere from 6,000 to 10,000 ads per day thanks to social media.

All of this is not to mention the countless news feeds, social media posts, and Zoom meetings you likely interact with every day as well.

Phew! No wonder you're exhausted!

Ethan Beute and Stephen Pacinelli refer to the cacophony of digital communications we receive every day as *digital pollution*, and they suggest that the costs of digital pollution include, among other things, "lost time, decreased productivity, heightened awareness, increased scrutiny, and reduced emotional well-being." I'll take that one step further to assert that this digital pollution can also negatively impact our relationships and our professional reputations.

Wait … our relationships and professional reputation … how so? Well, here's the thing. As frustrating as it can be to receive so much digital noise, you likely perpetuate it, too. How many times have you fired off an email, text, or IM without giving its clarity and/or impact on the reader much, if any, thought? How many times have you forwarded something to multiple people because *you* thought it was important, timely, or interesting, but not given much thought to inundating someone else's inbox? How many times have you sent an automated communique to colleagues or clients rather than personalizing it? How many times have you facilitated or participated in a meeting where your lack of preparation and/or attention wasted others' time?

Do you ever feel like people respond to your communications less often than they used to? Or perhaps their responses are frustratingly terse, abrupt, or confusing. Or perhaps they never respond at all.

It could be that they, too, are simply inundated. Again, we all are. But … it could be that your communications just aren't landing with any impact. Or worse, it could be that your communications are putting people off. Perhaps your communications are the ones that are frustratingly terse, abrupt, or confusing. Or perhaps *you* never respond at all.

Before I began working as a consultant in leadership development and communication skills, I was an academic. I have a Ph.D. in Human Communication Studies, and I was a communication professor and associate dean for a master's program at the University of Denver. This program is geared toward working adults, so our courses used to be held in person in the evenings. About twenty years ago, the program I taught for had just recently begun to offer some courses online. Now, of course, many programs are fully online or hybrid, but back then it was a brand-new concept!

One day during this time, I was having a conversation with a professor in a department called Digital Media Studies (it has since changed monikers). This colleague's name was Jeff, and he asked me how I felt about the fact that we were beginning to offer online courses. As you can probably surmise from the title of the department he worked for, he was what I'll call "pro-IT." I told him in no uncertain terms that I wasn't a fan. And I had no desire to teach any online courses—not now, not ever.

He asked with genuine curiosity, "Why not?" And I said, "Because I teach **human** communication. That means I study and teach how humans communicate and interact with one another."

Without missing a beat, Jeff said, "That *is* how humans communicate and interact with one another."

"Whoa," I thought, "he's right."

I made up my mind right then that I needed to teach online but, more importantly, I needed to do it well because I never wanted the online medium to be a barrier to ensuring that my students were actually learning.

Why am I telling you this story? Because I think many people today (perhaps including you) view the use of the online medium as justification for poor communication skills. They make the argument in their minds that virtual and digital communication somehow don't count as communication, that it's okay if we communicate less clearly, more abruptly, less responsively, and with more errors than when we communicate in person.

And I'm suggesting to you that nothing could be further from the truth.

This book is about a concept I call *computer-side manner*™. I coined that term to illustrate the notion that, nowadays, we cannot separate the way we communicate electronically from the way we communicate in person. Think about a highly skilled doctor. From the patient's perspective, their bedside manner is equally important (if not more so) than their medical knowledge. A doctor's bedside manner impacts the extent to which a patient trusts them, listens to them, and puts faith in their medical knowledge. Your computer-side manner is analogous to the doctor's bedside manner; your communication illustrates the holistic picture of Who You Are. Your computer-side manner is how you show up in digital spaces—all of them. This is true regardless of the medium or channel.

And with that in mind, what does your communication say about you? Think about it. Your communication **is** your brand. And there is no time in which this is not true.

Your communication is a direct reflection of who you are. Some theorists might go so far as to argue your communication **is** who you are. We don't need to get that philosophical, but suffice it to say, your communication has immediate short- and long-term impacts on how other people understand you, perceive you, think about you, interact with you, and value you, or not.

In today's world, many people know you only by your digital communication. So, your reputation literally precedes you—and not always in a good way. When you've already established a reputation, your communication is received and acted on based on that reputation.

So, pause right now and give some thought to your communication skills. On a scale of 1–10, how would you rate them? Ask yourself:

- How do I talk to others in person?
- How do I listen to others in person?
- How do I talk to others in Zoom meetings?
- How do I listen in Zoom meetings?
- How do I communicate by email?
- How do I communicate by Slack or Teams?
- How do I update progress reports?
- How do I update support tickets?
- How do I write reports?
- How do I create slide decks?
- How do I present information in meetings?

Yes. All of this counts as communication. And guess what? It all matters. Yep, all of it. Oh, I know what you're thinking— no, no, Slack and Teams don't count. Oh, but they do. But let's put a pin in that specific piece for now. We'll return to it later.

People have accepted the fact that, nowadays, there is little to no delineation between a person's professional and personal persona. People want to see individuals and companies as real, authentic, and genuine. Eighty-six percent of consumers say they look for authenticity in brands, meaning they want transparency and authenticity in how companies present themselves and carry out their business. But this doesn't just apply to organizations. Due to the increased blurring of the lines between personal and professional personas nowadays, you are your brand. This is not just true of solopreneurs and small-business owners. You represent both yourself and your organization, whether owned by you or someone else, 100 percent of the time.

Think about the countless stories of people losing their jobs due to something they posted on social media. A quick Google search will reveal many stories, such as the one about sportscaster Damian Goddard's firing for making homophobic tweets. His employer was not a fan of his sharing his personal opinions about gay marriage, and he was summarily let go.

That same line that has been blurred between your personal and professional personas has now been blurred, if not altogether removed, between how you communicate in person and how you show up online. You have to talk the talk **and** walk the walk.

I can't tell you how many times I have had people complain to me about how others communicate, only to turn around and communicate poorly with me themselves. (Honestly, it's countless.) I think this is because people don't understand that your communication is a holistic concept. It's about how you approach your interactions with people **every single time**, in **every single context**.

Let's look at important numbers that give these ideas some legs.

Research studies from Harvard University, the Carnegie Foundation, and Stanford Research Center have all found that 85 percent of job success comes from soft skills like communication, while only 15 percent comes from technical skills and knowledge. This is true even in IT fields.

Think about how many start-ups don't make it. If you drill down, you'll see that the majority of the time it's not that the idea or concept wasn't solid; it's that the IT guru who had the initial idea didn't have the communication and leadership skills (of which communication skills are a critical component) to lead the company well. The ones who make it do so either because they were smart enough to hire people to help with employee management or because they actually do have strong communication skills.

Entrepreneur Magazine calls poor communication one of the top five reasons why start-up leaders fail the company. And Steve Wozniak said in an interview that one of the main reasons for Steve Jobs's success with Apple was his "relentless drive to become a better communicator" because Steve Jobs knew how critical it was to motivate and inspire his employees.

When asked what best defines the "gap" in the US workforce skills gap, 42 percent of managers surveyed named soft skills, while only 22 percent named technical skills.

Let's consider the impact that these gaps in communication skills have in and on organizations.

Four hundred surveyed corporations estimated that communication barriers cost the average organization $62.4 million per year in lost productivity.

A business with 100 employees spends an average of seventeen hours per week clarifying communication. This amounts to an annual loss of just over $528,000.

A staggering 86 percent of employees and executives cite the lack of effective collaboration and communication as the main causes of workplace failures.

Eighty percent of employees say effective communication is a major factor in building trust in their employer; however, only 32 percent of employees rate their leaders' communication positively. And without that trust, approximately 50 percent of employees will actively search for another job.

Now maybe you're thinking, "OK, but these are broad-based statistics." I understand. Sometimes it can be hard to envision how data like these illustrate anything about you personally.

So, let's also look at it from an individual perspective.

Research illustrates time and time again that your communication skills say so much more about you than you realize—or likely more than you intend. People make inferences about you based on your communication skills.

They make inferences about:

- Your level of education
- Your level of intelligence
- Your pride in your work
- Your credibility
- Your business expertise

Again, this is all about inferences. You may have an advanced degree, and you may be an expert at what you do, but if you can't articulate that, it does you no good because people have only one thing to go on—how you communicate those things.

And in today's litigious and divisive culture, most people won't tell you that your communication skills need work. They'll just adjust how they interact with you.

I want to ask you to think back over the span of your working life. I'll start with a simple question: How many resumes did you send out that you never got responses to?

I once received a resume from a woman applying for a project leader position at my university. Her resume touted her "extreme attention to detail" but then, only two lines below, said she could provide "References upo request." Attention to detail? Hmmm … I don't think so.

Now, you may ask, people will seriously discount what otherwise might be a good candidate over one mistake?

The answer: Yes, some people will. I did.

But let's look way past resumes.

Think of how many other possible opportunities didn't come to fruition and you never knew why. Here's a checklist. Take a look at these questions and answer with as much honest self-reflection as you can.

Again, think back over the span of your working life:

- Have you ever sent an email to someone about an opportunity that might have moved you ahead, but it never came to fruition?

- Have you ever been asked by someone else to revise, clarify, or explain something you've written? More than once? Multiple times? Frequently?

- Has someone ever responded to you by saying something like, "Um, I asked you three questions and you only answered one of them"?

- Has a difficult situation with a colleague or client ever escalated due to your words—written or spoken?

- Have you ever just felt that your potential isn't being recognized? Perhaps you've languished too long in the same role and feel your seniority or skill should have earned you more advancement.

- Here's one more. Have you ever finished a project you were proud of that got little to no recognition or traction? Maybe you knocked an API out of the park, but it didn't move the needle with your boss? Or you finished a brand-new integration that was unique, but no one noticed? If yes, it is wholly likely that these were because you did not effectively articulate the value of these things.

If you've said "yes" to any of these, then it is likely that your communication skills have had an impact in a way you might not have realized.

And when you reflect on your communication skills, you need to take a 360-degree view of your communication. You need to examine how you articulate your thoughts in every context—how you show up as a communicator.

Communication is ubiquitous, and yet it's something that too few of us give enough thought to—at least, not to our own.

Be honest (this book is going to be all about being honest with yourself!): how often have you complained about or even made fun of poor communication on someone else's part? Now, how often have you turned that mirror toward yourself to examine your own communication effectiveness?

It can be a tough thing to admit that our communication skills may be, ahem, less than perfect. And even when we are brave enough to turn the spotlight on ourselves, it can be easy to rationalize or justify our communication behaviors.

"I was in a hurry."
"I hadn't had my coffee yet."
"I'm not an English major."
"She knows not to push my buttons like that."
"They'll understand what I meant."
"I don't need to be that picky."
"I'm too busy to follow up."
"I'm too busy to give that a second read-through."
"I'm too busy to pay attention in this meeting."
(The "I'm too busy" excuse comes up a lot!)

But these are all just excuses. And if you've bought this book, then you already inherently know what I'm about to tell you—these excuses are BS.

And here's why. Because the person on the receiving end of your ill-conceived, ill-timed, poorly executed, rude, confusing, unclear, or otherwise ineffective communication doesn't give a rip about any of these excuses. They only care how your communication affects **them**.

In a world full of digital pollution, if you're not part of the solution you're part of the pollution.

And what's more, as the title of this book suggests, if people see you as part of the problem contributing to their digital pollution, then this is likely holding you back professionally, and maybe personally, too.

Let me share a real example. A colleague of mine whom I'll call Brendan recently started a local networking group for IT leaders in his industry-specific niche. Brendan sent a blurb about the group with an invite to join to many of his current and former colleagues. He received this actual email response from one of his contacts, with whom he had worked at a previous company:

"I don't know what this has to do with me or what I do. I'm not even in IT."

The response was clearly abrupt, but it was also odd since, as far as Brendan knew, this person was in IT. It turned out that this man was between jobs, but Brendan would have had no way of knowing that. So, this man's response was unnecessarily impolite. And, as it turns out, it ended up biting him in the posterior. How so? Just a couple of weeks later, Brendan's company was hiring, and this man reached out to Brendan directly to inquire about the position. Need I tell you how likely it was that Brendan hired him?

You just never know when communication that you may have given little thought to (but should have) or that you wrote off as being "good enough" will have a real-life negative impact on your relationships and/or your career.

I don't want that for you! So, this book aims to introduce you to the most common mistakes people make in their digital communication. As you read each chapter, ask yourself the tough question: are you making this mistake? If not, great! You can skip that chapter. But read the next one. Because you're likely making some, if not most, of the mistakes because, well, you're human, and most humans do.

But the good news is that the book will also outline solutions to these mistakes. Many of the solutions I'll teach you are grounded in brain science. Now, wait! Don't put the book down if I just scared you with the words "brain science." You don't have to know the brain science—that's my job—but if you geek out on it as I do, you'll love those parts! These strategies are easy to employ—I promise! The science allows me to explain to you why the strategies work.

The strategies in this book are also informed by my years of communication expertise. Since I earned my Ph.D. in Human Communication Studies nearly twenty years ago, I've spent the proceeding years teaching undergraduate students and graduate students; clients from corporations and nonprofits; and members of professional associations how to communicate better. I've heard every communication problem, every miscommunication, and every excuse for poor communication you can imagine. In this book, I will share what I've witnessed in my twenty years of teaching and consulting, and the strategies that have been successful for my students and my clients.

This book will open your mind to some things you may not have realized about how your communication skills, or lack thereof, are having an impact on your professional persona and relationships. And if you do the work, this book will provide you with easy-to-implement tools and strategies for becoming fully confident in your ability to be a more impactful communicator.

What do I mean by "impactful communicator"? Granted, "impactful" is one of those words that can tend to be overused, and usually hyperbolically—kind of like the way people call everything "awesome" or "perfect" nowadays. Oh, my coffee's ready? Awesome! Your name is spelled S-M-I-T-H? Perrrrfect.

I digress … so, how am I using "impactful? Well … not as hyperbole! By "impactful," I mean that your communication accomplishes what you want it to accomplish. By impactful, I mean that your digital communication is not just technically well-written, but also achieves its goals.

Think about it: nearly all, if not all, of your professional communications are begun with a goal in mind. Whether that goal is to build rapport, establish a relationship, gain a client, communicate a policy, share news, update status, or request information, the truth is that not every communication interaction you engage in (write, send, provide, say, etc.) achieves what you hope or think it will.

So, the goal of this book is to teach you to craft impactful communication so that anytime you communicate with another person, you achieve what you want to achieve, which in turn, will cultivate your reputation as an effective communicator.

When that happens, you'll no longer be a digital polluter; you'll be a digital enhancer! And when people see you as enhancing communication interactions, they'll look forward to interacting with you. They'll view you as a highly effective communicator, and your professional reputation will be much stronger.

Are you ready to begin? Great!

Chapter 2

MISTAKE #1: THINKING YOUR INDUSTRY KNOWLEDGE IS THE ONLY THING THAT MATTERS

I once had an IT developer say to me, "I'm in IT. It doesn't matter how well I communicate, only how well I code."

Trust me when I tell you that how you communicate may matter less to you than it should, but it matters a whole lot to your peers and your leadership.

- Do you wish to advance in your career?

- Do you want to be admired for your work, not just what you produce, but your *work*—meaning, how you do your work, not just what you produce?
- Do you wish to have positive relationships with the people you work with?

If you've said "yes" to any of those things, this chapter is critical for you. Only a true misanthrope who also has no concern for relationships, professional reputation, or professional advancement should embrace the philosophy that your communication doesn't matter.

Let me share a true, and recent, story of a person who made the mistake of thinking his communication skills didn't matter because he was a good coder.

A colleague of mine—let's call him Julius—was in an IT leadership position for a company in which he supervised a team of twelve or so developers. One of his developers, in Julius's words, wrote "absolutely beautiful code." But he had to fire him anyway. Why?

Because this developer—let's call him Burt—suffered from poor communication skills that hurt the team. Julius explained to me that most talented coders are extremely focused while coding—head down, blinders on, the rest of the world ceases to exist. This is great while you're coding, but it's not fruitful to take that kind of approach to being a good employee or colleague.

According to Julius, though Burt was an excellent coder, he neglected to properly communicate what he was doing in a way that helped the rest of the team. He failed to communicate to

Julius or the team what he was creating or updating, why he was working on it, and what part of the project it was for.

Burt's lack of communication was highly problematic for Julius. Julius's job is to manage the projects on which the team is working and to ensure that the projects are completed on time, in the most efficient manner possible, and on budget. Burt's lack of communication left Julius in a bind constantly because Julius had no idea what percentage of the project's components Burt had completed. He had no insight into whether Burt was writing any code that could or should be shared with other members of the team so that they didn't have to write the same pieces of code to perform the same function he was working on. What happened, as a result, is that the team frequently *did* write code for the same functions Burt was working on. This caused the project to take longer to complete than they had promised the client, which also meant it was over budget.

It also meant that any future updates would automatically take longer because duplicate code would require that any changes in the future be made in multiple places.

There were two avenues of communication that Burt should have used to set his team up for success. First, he should have communicated to Julius and his team what he was working on. He too rarely did this, and even when he did, his updates lacked clarity and context; so, in effect, they were useless. Second, he should have documented what he had done, both internally and externally. This would have allowed team members to search for that functionality on their own if Burt had neglected to proactively communicate that he had worked on it.

But he did neither.

As a result, Julian was frustrated because he could not properly do his job to ensure streamlined processes, eliminate redundancies, and ensure that projects are on budget and on time. The client was frustrated because not only was the project late and over budget but also the team had, in effect, not written "good code" due to the multiple redundancies in the code. And finally, the team was frustrated because Burt's lack of communication efforts, despite repeated coaching, impaired their ability to do their jobs well; it also led to relational tensions because it created a constant game of "whose code is better?" when redundant code was created.

The ultimate result? Despite the fact that Burt was a "beautiful coder," he was let go.

The moral of this story is that effective communication doesn't just mean writing things without typos. Remember that we're talking about your computer-side manner—the holistic picture of who you are as a communicator. It's how you "show up" in your computer-mediated communication.

It is through communication, *not technical skills*, that you present your professional persona, brand, and reputation to the world around you.

Whether you're in IT or financial services, real estate or the medical field, your technical skills and knowledge are important, to be sure. But they are not everything; some would argue they're not even the most important thing. You may think you're one of the best CPAs or financial advisors out there, but (a) I assure you there are thousands more just as good as you, and (b) if you can't communicate your analysis effectively, it doesn't matter how good the technical skills are; you won't have as many clients as someone who is good at communicating and good at building relationships.

> "The term *soft skills* diminishes the importance of communication—like the term *free* diminishes the value of something. But these skills are critical. Without strong written and verbal communication skills, the expertise doesn't matter because no one understands what you do, and all people can focus on is how you show up. No one wants to spend time listening to someone "smart" if they don't get you. If we're bringing you in because you're the expert, that means it's on you to bring others along."
> ~Gretchen Schott, Chief Learning Office at Threefold

I recently had a conversation with the Chief Information Officer (CIO) of a company in Indianapolis. He told me that his biggest frustration with his role is that people in his world focus on the technical aspects of their jobs to the detriment of the human side. Even those, he suggested, who are really good at what they do fail to understand that it's still *humans* who have to explain, champion, and implement the technology. When the communication behind the technology breaks down, the technology will be viewed as a failure. But all too often, it's just that the communication *about* the technology is what failed. This CIO lamented that too few of his people can articulate the value of the technology, create champions for it, foster collaboration behind how to use it well, and foster strong relationships with those who use it—especially those who may struggle with it. But all those things have to take place for the technology itself to be a success! Leaders need their team members to be good communicators, not just good technicians.

And speaking of leaders, think about every good leader you've ever heard about or known personally. Are they considered good leaders because of their knowledge? Or, at least, **only** because of their knowledge? Not likely. The best leaders in the world are typically considered so because of their communication skills. But communication skills sort of live in the shadows, so it's not a person's communication per se that we tend to notice. When someone is a good communicator, we don't necessarily notice how they communicate, but what we do notice is how they make us feel, how they foster and facilitate, how they support and listen, and how they follow through.

Take astronaut Scott Kelly, for example. He emerged as an excellent leader of the International Space Station (ISS) crew. Before spending almost a year on the ISS, Kelly was a twenty-year veteran who had already flown four missions to space, so his technical knowledge was evident. It would have been easy for him to ride (pun intended) those skills to the finish. But he took it one step further and emerged as a leader for the crew by working with his international compatriots to find common ground and build objectives they all bought into and, thus, achieved. The impact he made as a leader (not to mention the data he provided furthering our knowledge of the impact of space travel on humans) is evident in his best-selling book.

To be fair, not everyone wishes to be a leader. But everyone who has any type of career is a spokesperson for their organization, no matter what their role. Whether you own your own business or work for a 5,000-employee organization, you are a representative of that organization when you interact with colleagues, clients, investors, media, social media, etc. Think about this: if you call Zappos and have a bad experience with one of their customer service representatives—let's say her name is Stacy—you don't say, "Oh gosh, poor Stacy seems to be having a bad day," or even "Stacy wasn't very helpful." You say, "Zappos has terrible customer service." You name the company, not the person.

And so do most people. This is why you are always on the hot seat to represent yourself and your organization well through your communication.

Any one employee's poor communication skills can lead to many negative effects on an organization's ability to succeed, such as:

- **Lost Business:** If you don't handle a situation with strong and effective written communication, all your customer has to do is hop onto Google and contact your competitor. This leads to a lack of business growth.
- **Lost Productivity:** If you don't take the time up front to ensure clarity and a positive tone in communications, you waste your and others' time. Communications that lack clarity or have a poor tone all too often have to be clarified, rewritten, discussed, and sometimes remediated. This all takes time away from work that could move your project forward.
- **No Advocates:** If you don't clearly communicate what your business does and how it can help, how can you

expect outside people to tell their friends, family, coworkers, and others about the business? It won't happen. The message needs to be clear, concise, and presented effectively. With a strong message, outsiders will be able to spread the word and drive more business to you. Without clear communication about your business, your competitors have the advantage.

These are just a few of the effects of ignoring poor communication skills as a result of assuming industry knowledge is all that matters.

But fret not! It's not all gloom and doom. The good news is that research also illustrates that professionals with effective writing skills see tangible returns on those efforts, which means you can develop better communication skills to increase your effectiveness.

Consider, for example, a Grammarly.com study of 100 LinkedIn profiles. In the same ten-year period, professionals who received six to nine promotions made 55 percent fewer grammatical errors than professionals who were promoted only one to four times during the same period. The same study also found that professionals who had reached senior-level positions within ten years made 2.5 times fewer grammatical errors than colleagues who had failed to move to that level of leadership.

Consistently across all studies, people report that others' effective writing skills communicate intelligence, professionalism, and competency. And people report making positive assumptions about others' intellectual aptitude, attention to detail, and critical thinking skills if they demonstrate effective writing skills.

Perhaps you're not motivated by career growth or becoming a leader. Perhaps you're totally happy right where you are. That's fair. But I'll assume that, even if that's true, you want to keep your job. I'll remind you of my story about Burt from earlier in the chapter and tell you another true story. At a previous job I held, I was in a leadership position. There was a young woman on the team I led who was responsible for tracking and compiling our data and providing basic analysis of trends to share with our regional leadership. Because the rest of my team was not as skilled in data analysis, we needed her to be good at communicating to us what tactics she used to track and compile the data, how it was being represented, etc. I want to say that she was good at the technical part of her job. But the truth is, I can't be sure if she was good at the technical aspect of her job because her communication skills were so poor that, not only could she not communicate her process and her findings, but she also got frustrated that she was even being asked to. She would send my team the data and, when I would email her to ask her to meet with the team to walk through it with us, she would respond with terse responses like, "I sent you the report. The information is already there."

Despite repeated coaching from me as well as her direct supervisor, she was unwilling or unable (I suppose we'll never know) to improve her communication—her approach as well as her skills. So, unfortunately, we eventually had to let her go.

The next part of this story might seem farcical, but I assure you it's true. The job she had with us was this young woman's first technical job and, since she could not rely on us for a reference, she was unable to find another one. So, she got a job as an assistant dog groomer. Now, there's nothing whatsoever wrong with being an assistant dog groomer if that's what one wishes to do. I have great respect for anyone with that level of skill and patience! But I know it was not the job she really wanted because she ran into one of her former teammates one day and asked if he thought we might hire her back. The answer, I'm afraid, was no.

So, perhaps I've convinced you to, in theory, eliminate the false delineation between your industry knowledge and your communication skills; you agree with me now that they're not mutually exclusive. But perhaps you think, "But Ali, I'm just not like that. I'm just *not* a good communicator."

To that, I say "rubbish," to borrow a word I love from our British compatriots. Is it true that some people are naturally more gifted at communication than others? Sure, I'll readily grant you that. But it is not true that you, or anyone with standard cognitive abilities, are incapable of improving your communication skills.

Just like any skill, it takes first, the commitment to get better at it. Second, it takes work and practice. If you don't practice communicating more effectively, you will not get better at it. Public speaking coach Alex Perry uses a great analogy when she compares communication skills to having six-pack abs. Sure, you might want six-pack abs, but if you eat Cheetos every day, you're making a choice that is going to take you further away from those abs. Or maybe you had a six-pack once. That doesn't mean you get to say, "Great! I finally have that six-pack. Now I can finally stop eating healthfully and exercising." You still have to make those choices pretty much every day. Communication is no different. It's about making a conscious choice, every time you communicate with someone in any medium, and to do so effectively—that is, clearly, concisely, and with a positive tone (at a minimum).

So, how do you get there? I'm going to share some more tangible and universal tips for effective communication choices later. But for now, let me address how you can move from thinking either "my communication skills don't matter" or "I'm just not a good communicator" to "*I can do this!*"

Josh Kaufman, author of *The First 20 Hours: How to Learn Anything … Fast!,* says (you may have guessed this from the title) that you can learn any new skill in twenty hours. Twenty hours—that's it!

Josh notes that most people are dissuaded from continuing the pursuit of learning new skills because they are not good at them at first, and that feels discouraging. So, the easiest way to feel better is to quit trying. Plus, it feels incredibly daunting to set about "mastering" a new skill. So, his advice and I concur—is to forget about mastering the skill, and just commit to learning how to do it. Commit to putting in at least twenty hours of practice of the new skill (in this case, the approaches I'll share later to improve your communication skills). Twenty hours is nothing in the big scheme of things. That's one hour a day for twenty days. That's hard work and commitment, for sure, but totally doable. It turns out that there are cognitive reasons why twenty is the magic number here. The following quote from a *Forbes* interview with Kaufman explains this beautifully:

"Numerous studies in the fields of motor and cognitive skill acquisition have established that the first few hours of practicing a new skill always generate the most dramatic improvements in performance.

The general pattern looks like this: when you start, you're horrible, but you improve very quickly as you learn the most important parts of the skill. After reaching a certain level of skill very quickly, your rate of improvement declines, and subsequent improvement becomes much slower.

In the research literature, this phenomenon is referred to as the 'power law of practice,' and it's one of the most consistent findings in skill acquisition research. The effect has been widely known since at least 1926, and it's been replicated many times since in studies of both physical and mental skills. One study I found ("Toward an Instance Theory of Automatization," G. D. Logan, Psychological Review, 1988) even went so far as to say, 'Any theory of skill acquisition that does not accommodate the power law function for learning can be rejected immediately.'

The exact amount of time it takes to acquire a new skill depends on your desired performance level. If you don't make things harder than they really need to be, it's not at all uncommon to reach your initial objective in a few hours. For example, I learned enough about yoga in three hours to be able to practice safely at home. Given what I wanted to learn, that was enough.

The twenty-hour threshold comes from combining the power law of practice with insights from behavioral psychology and game theory. Pre-committing to twenty hours of practice does a few important things:

It's an important indicator of how important the skill really is to you right now. If you're not willing to rearrange your schedule to make time for practice, or you're not willing to invest that much time to get what you want, it's a good indicator the skill really isn't that important to you at the moment, so you're better off choosing to do something else.

Making a serious pre-commitment to practice at least twenty hours before acting at all helps overcome the slippery slope of procrastination. Instead of saying 'I'll get to it later,' the pre-commitment serves as a variation of what's called a 'Schelling point,' which pressures you to behave in a manner that's consistent with your pre-commitment. It's a line in the sand designed to influence your behavior in the moment, so you actually practice.

> Twenty hours is long enough to experience dramatic improvements in skill, but not so long that it feels too overwhelming to get started in the first place."

Joseph Weintraub, a professor of management and organizational behavior at Babson College and co-author of the book, *The Coaching Manager: Developing Top Talent in Business*, also has some helpful suggestions about learning new skills. First, he suggests that you should check your readiness when you are preparing to learn a new skill; for example, assess the importance of that skill to you, and ask yourself whether the timing is right for this endeavor. The commitment to learning it is paramount; without it, you are unlikely to succeed.

Second, he suggests you should make sure the skill is relevant for you; that is, do you need it in your professional and/or personal life? Do others around you (your manager, e.g.) value that skill? Would they support your taking the time to improve it? If you're reading this book, then I will safely assume the answers to these questions are a resounding "yes."

And finally, Dr. Weintraub also suggests you get support along the way. Bring one or two trusted colleagues into the fold to let them know you're working on your communication skills, and ask them if you can check in with them in routine intervals to see how they think you're doing. Accountability is an important part of making a commitment, and talking with others about what you're learning and doing helps you cement positive change.

I hope this chapter has sparked that sense of commitment in you and that I've left little doubt that it's a mistake to assume that your industry knowledge is enough to sustain a successful career. Whether you want to advance in your field or simply be respected and earn financial rewards for your work, you must round out your industry knowledge with effective communication skills. And the good news is that it is possible to build these skills—all it takes is a bit of proverbial elbow grease!

Chapter 3

MISTAKE #2:
THINKING THAT THE ONUS IS ON THE OTHER PERSON TO FIGURE OUT WHAT YOU MEAN WHEN YOUR COMMUNICATION IS UNCLEAR OR POORLY WRITTEN

hen we engage in interactions with other people, every exchange is a two-way street. We are the sender at the moment that we are the person talking or writing, and the receiver at the moment we are the one listening or reading. The onus for clear communication is always—repeat ALWAYS—on the sender.

My husband and I just built a house. This is a real excerpt from a real email exchange I had with a vendor we were trying to work with. I had already emailed him several times about meeting and gotten no response. So, I emailed him again, and the following exchange took place:

> **Me:** Rob, just reaching out to see if you are available to meet this week. As a reminder, we are available Thursday or Friday between two and four each day. Thanks!
>
> **Rob:** Yes, that could work.
>
> **Me:** Rob, I'm sorry, can you clarify? Which day and at exactly which time would you like to meet?
>
> **Rob:** 3:00 is great.
>
> **Me:** Rob, I initially offered Thursday or Friday between 2–4. Can you please be specific as to the day AND time we can meet? Thank you.

This may seem like a small example, but (a) this exchange illustrates only about 1 percent of the frustrating exchanges both my builder and I had with this person and (b) each time we had an exchange like this, my time was wasted and my frustration grew. So, the outcome? Neither my builder nor I will work with this person again. And I've shared my experience with friends who were looking for this type of vendor, meaning he is not receiving referrals from me.

Unfortunately, this exchange illustrates the all-too-common mistake for which this chapter is titled. Perhaps I should have listed this as mistake #1 because I think it may be the most pervasive one. I find that many people genuinely believe that it is the responsibility of the recipient to make sense of their communication. Nothing could be further from the truth. **The onus, 100 percent of the time, is on the communicator.**

And this isn't just my opinion. This is science.

Most of the time when you communicate with others, you have a particular goal for that interaction. Whether that goal is to persuade someone to do you a favor, build rapport, establish a relationship, gain a client, communicate a policy, share news, request information, or even just express support or interest, most communicative interactions have some type of goal. However, those goals will not be met if you don't connect with the other person when you communicate with them.

What do I mean by "connect with the other person"? I don't mean this in a touchy-feely sort of way, as in, "Look into my eyes and connect with me." Not that there's anything wrong with that; I highly recommend it! But in this case, I'm referring to the fact that cognitively speaking, for understanding to take place, you have to literally connect to something that already exists in the other person's brain.

Let's explore.

The brain is comprised of approximately 100 billion neurons or brain cells. Some scientists say it's much higher—even into the trillions. These cells contain nuclei, which make enzymes, proteins, and neurotransmitters; these are the chemicals necessary for the nerve cells in the brain to communicate with one another. Neurons have a single axon, which is a long tube that sends electrical impulses—called *action potentials*—to other cells. You can think of an axon like Harry Potter's wand.

Neurons also have dendrites, which are more complicated structures; they are basically like little hands, which *receive* electrical impulses from the axon terminals of other neurons.

A synapse is a specialized site at which the communication between two neurons happens. A synapse is a junction created between two neurons when an action potential causes the creation and release of a neurotransmitter, which is a chemical reaction caused by the action potential having traveled down the axon. The Queensland Brain Institute notes that "synapses can be thought of as converting an electrical signal (the action potential) into a chemical signal in the form of neurotransmitter release, and then, upon binding of the transmitter to the postsynaptic receptor, switching the signal back again into an electrical form, as charged ions flow into or out of the postsynaptic neuron."

So, we have the axon, dendrite, and synapse. These things come together to form what's called a *neuronal network*.

As amazing as these neuronal networks sound, what's even more amazing is how they function. Neuronal networks are knowledge. As James Zull notes, it's not just that they store knowledge. They do, but this is an incomplete picture. They ARE knowledge. Every time we *learn* something new—not every time we simply hear or read something, but every time learning actually takes place—a synaptic connection is made, and a new one of these tiny little branches is formed.

You can think of the brain as comprised of trillions (yep, trillions) of tiny little storage cubbies—like the ones you used in kindergarten. Each thing you've ever learned is stored in one of those cubbies. Anytime you encounter new data or stimuli, your brain immediately starts searching these cubbies to ask, "How is this new thing like something I already know?"

So, learning—i.e., growing more synaptic connections—must come from a *physical* change in our neuronal networks, which means that new information must be connected to an existing neuronal network—in other words, to existing knowledge.

How does that happen?

When stimuli enter our brain in the form of an electrical impulse, we don't process all stimuli the same way. Some data is processed with a low-level, weaker signal, and some with a high-level, stronger signal. The latter will result in a stronger synaptic connection, which is more likely to be turned into long-term memory.

What makes the difference in whether we process data with a weak or strong signal? Prior experience.

When a person has prior experience with incoming data, this leads to a stronger synaptic connection to that data. Less or no experience leads to a feeble connection. Only strong synaptic connections are turned into long-term memory; thus, with feeble connections, no understanding can occur because the connection is ultimately lost.

This means that understanding, and subsequently, long-term changes like learning, cannot take place without that synaptic connection—without the formation of a new neuronal network in the brain. And remember that this connection is a real, physical structure in the brain—a neuronal pathway.

So, all this is to say that when you communicate with other people, if you're not finding a way to connect to their prior knowledge, you are not facilitating their understanding of your message. And if they don't understand your message, your communication goal for that interaction is not going to be accomplished.

> "I have hordes of examples of email chains that all took place because the first email was a poorly written statement lacking clarity. In the case of compliance, it leads to confusion and assumptions (not always positive assumptions), rework, and, in a few cases, extra costs of thousands of dollars in re-reporting and submittals. In the more generic way, it [also] leads to way too many emails, confused reporting to different leadership chains, and a massive amount of labor doing damage control. The main thing I share with my team is to never assume—because the devil is in the details."
>
> ~ Jason Clifford, Assistant Vice President,
> AHS AMER Product Development for dormakaba

This further drives home the point that you can't just assume that communication is simply "putting it out there" and making the recipient do all the work. That's just broadcasting; it's not communication. Communication is a two-way street; by *definition,* it must involve the sender *and* the receiver.

A colleague of mine who leads a team in the healthcare industry told me one of his employees struggles with this common mistake. He told me, "He sends things to the team seemingly with the singular goal of getting it off his plate. There is no regard for whether his communication accomplishes anything. Consequently, I spend too much of my time trying to make sense of his ramblings. As of late, I find myself having to defend why I haven't taken action about his consistent lack of clarity, and everyone is frustrated with me now. I am at the end of my rope, frankly."

As I said earlier, I believe this may be the single-most common communication mistake—thinking that once you have spoken or written, your job is done.

I want you to think back to high school or college. Try to remember the worst teacher you ever had, not one you didn't like because you got a bad grade, but a teacher from whom you genuinely felt you learned nothing. Now try to remember the best teacher you ever had. What was the biggest difference between them? I'm guessing that the worst teacher followed the old sage-on-the-stage model. She or he lectured at you. Perhaps she or he used a lot of big words, textbook definitions, and explanations. We know from research that the "sage-on-the-stage" approach to teaching doesn't engender learning. This is true for two reasons that are related but distinct. First, the sage-on-the-stage model of teaching doesn't work because it doesn't involve the learner. It's akin to the professor saying, "I'm the expert. I'll share my knowledge, but it's up to you to figure out what it means and what to do with it." Second, low-frequency activities like lecturing allow the listener's brain to stay at lower levels of cognitive development.

Now think back to the best teacher you ever had. I'm guessing he or she involved the class a lot. He or she probably asked as many questions of you as you did him or her. Therefore, it's much more likely that learning took place.

When you simply dole out your information with the expectation that it's the recipient's responsibility to figure it out, rather than your responsibility to make it clear, you are that "worst" teacher. When you treat every communication interaction as a partnership, a collaboration—*we're in this together, and I'm going to make this as easy as possible for you*—then you're that "best" teacher!

As I mentioned in Chapter 2, I'll offer more universal tips for enhancing your computer-side manner later in the book. But for now, let's look at some strategies to help you avoid making the mistake of assuming it's up to your reader to make sense of your communication.

The trick is to always write with your recipient in mind—that is, try to ensure that you are being clear and concise and providing the appropriate context. Remember that the onus is on you to make sure what you're saying is clear and concise. The onus is not on them to figure it out if you don't.

Some tips for how to do that:

- Remind people about what you're referencing. Don't expect that just because you remember "that conversation we had the other day," they also do. Be specific. Which day? Which conversation? What cues can you offer them to help re-connect to that conversation? Whenever possible, forward the email that contains the conversation you're referencing so they don't have to take the time to hunt for it on their own if they need to refresh their memory.

- Related to the previous bullet but specific to emails, be specific with your email subject lines. Rather than a subject line with vague wording like "My comments" or "An idea," use something like, "Thoughts for tomorrow's 9 am meeting" or "Follow-up to June 13 meeting," etc. Specific subject lines are incredibly helpful to your readers when they are looking through emails and/ or looking for a specific email so that they can more easily home in on what they're looking for.

- Be as specific as you can with your word choice. If you mean 1:00, don't say "early afternoon" because that could lead to a miscommunication whereby you meant 1:00 but your recipient infers 2:30. If you're talking about something where ninety minutes makes a difference, clarity matters. I once missed a meeting with a colleague because we agreed to meet at the "new building" on campus. She went to one new building, and I went to another one. I should have been specific with my word choice and named the building.

- Don't overuse pronouns. Too many pronouns confuse your recipient. Specify your referents. For example, if "it" could refer to more than one thing in your sentence, use the word for that thing rather than "it."

  - Instead of this ... *Danielle said she requested that from Bridget weeks ago, but she didn't know if it was clear.* (To what does "that" refer? To whom does the second "she" refer? Danielle? Bridget? Someone else? To what does "it" refer? The project? Danielle's request?)

  - Say this ... *Danielle said that she asked Bridget to provide the data on the Indigo project weeks ago, but she wasn't sure if Bridget understood the request.*

- Don't ramble. No one (and I mean no one—not even people who love you) likes to read rambling thoughts. Remember that we're living in an age of digital pollution. People are overwhelmed. It is easier to lose their attention, and rambling or prattling on with no clear point is the single best way to do that. Joseph McCormack, author of *BRIEF: Making a Bigger Impact by Saying Less*, conducted research in which he found that 43 percent of people who received long-winded emails deleted or ignored them.

A young woman on a team I used to lead was rather infamous for her long, rambling emails. I once received an email like this from her after a meeting in which I asked for the team's input on whether to open our committee to other staff members.

Hi Ali,

I was thinking about our meeting earlier, and your request in our meeting, and I have some thoughts I wanted to share with you about that. I don't know if you remember, but you asked us to let you know if we thought we should open our committee meetings up to other [company name] staff members. I was thinking about that, and I don't know if we should. On one hand, it could allow for transparency—allowing others to see what we are discussing can create a sense of security because people will know what path we're on. But on the other hand—and I don't know if this is important, but it is my opinion—are we opening ourselves up to a more drawn-out and complicated process if we allow for that much oversight by whoever wants to come in? I mean, said another way, I just wonder if there is something to be said for the fact that these people have been chosen for this committee for a reason, and why should this committee be any different than any other committee? In other committees, we all get a chance to speak into their outcomes before they are final, but we aren't all involved through the whole process.

I was on a different committee last year that did this, and it didn't go well. Now, that could have just been that particular committee—I understand that you are leading this one, and we have pretty clear direction right now. But I do remember that opening that committee to others right in the middle of it really changed the dynamic of the committee. It just seems to me that we can't all be on every committee, you know?

I hope this makes sense, and I hope it's OK that I sent this. It's really just my opinion, so I'm open to what others think as well.

Thanks, Ali. I appreciate your listening.

Sincerely,
Jane

Believe me, this was a short email compared to some of hers! But it makes my point adequately. It would have been clearer, not to mention easier and faster for both of us, had she just written something like this:

Hi Ali,

Regarding your request in our meeting this morning about voting on whether we should open our committee meetings to other staff, my concern with doing this is that it may over-complicate things for us. Additionally, it is the norm at [company name] to share outcomes with others and allow them to provide feedback rather than involve people outside the committee in the entire process.

I appreciate your asking our opinions, and I'm certainly open to others.

Thanks, Ali.

Sincerely,
Jane

I don't mean to suggest this email is perfect, but it's more concise than the original version. When you send communications that aren't concise over and over, people do feel frustrated. They feel like you don't respect their time, and, consequently, those feelings can lead to relational tension. For example, in this case, the unfortunate truth is that this young woman's rambling emails were a near-constant source of tension. Many people in the office found them frustrating and, therefore, most people just stopped reading them. This would, in turn, frustrate Jane when it was evident during meetings or other interactions that some people had not read what she sent. It became a vicious cycle.

Effective communication is like electricity—as long as it's there, you may not pay much attention because everything is flowing smoothly. But, when the power goes off, you can't think of much else. Everything stops. Nothing makes sense. Communications have ceased. Turn the power back on with concise and precise communication.

One of the best ways to avoid rambling is to avoid preambles. It can be tempting to share the backstory of how and why you reached the thought, conclusion, or request you're writing about before you share that thought. But in digital communications, people want you to cut to the chase. What is the critical, need-to-know information? Start with that. It doesn't mean you can't share the backstory—what research you've conducted, what experiences led you to this point, etc.—just don't start with that. Use a journalistic style of writing called the *inverted pyramid*, where you begin with the need-to-know info, and then drill down into the details. If people are in a hurry and/or stop reading early, at least they have the critical information. If you keep their interest, then they can keep reading for more information.

Remember that your charge here is to avoid being a digital polluter. Writing more clearly and concisely is one of the most important things you can do to that end.

Chapter 4

MISTAKE #3: THINKING IM COMMUNICATION DOESN'T COUNT

We live in a world where almost everything is instantly attainable. We have instant coffee, instant rice, and now, instant messaging—essentially, the closest digital equivalent to talking (the original instant message).

Some food writers define instant food as any food requiring less than five minutes of preparation time. I suppose that's not a bad definition of an instant message either since, most likely if you're typing something that takes longer than five minutes, you'll put it in an email (or, for goodness' sake, just pick up the phone!). You might even say instant messages (IMs) are more like an "ultra-instant" food, which is anything taking less than one minute to prepare—think "just add water"—since most people spend only seconds on the average IM.

We live in a world where even our digital communication is instant. That can be great because it affords all manner of ease and accessibility. Instant messages allow us to connect with others more readily than with other modes of digital communication. And they can help eliminate the pain point of waiting for a response to an email to continue a task or project.

However, instant messages have a downside, and a pretty serious one at that: they are likely the type of digital communication most fraught with poor tone and lack of clarity.

Be honest; how many times have you thought, "It's just a Slack message" or "It's only a Teams IM. Who cares?"

I'll tell you who cares: the person on the receiving end who is put off by the abruptness or confused by the total lack of context.

It's time in this day and age to stop treating instant messages as though they don't count as communication. The medium has nothing to do with the importance or efficacy of your message.

"Many technical people are focused on delivering something—a service, a product, a feature, a solution, etc. Oftentimes they forget this is only half the equation and that communicating what you are going to do, how you did it, and what's left to do is of equal importance to the stakeholder. I especially see this in instant message communications: in an attempt at solving a problem as quickly as possible, engineers will often forget to acknowledge that they saw the question and communicate that they are going to look at the issue at hand, leaving the requester in the dark as to what's happening (if anything)."

~ Gabrielle Hendryx-Parker. CEO and co-founder of tech accelerator Six Feet Up

I'll review instant messaging as a whole before discussing its impact on communication effectiveness.

Let's first examine some of the more general downsides of instant messaging.

First, instant messages are much harder to keep a record of and keep track of. Most IM systems allow you to search through the chat history to find previous communications; however, this would presuppose you remembered whom you were chatting with and which thread to search since most of us IM the same person via multiple threads—one may be a one-on-one channel between you and that person, but you may also have other group-chat channels involving that person. And even if you can find the message in question, organizing IMs in any meaningful fashion would take quite a bit of manual work on your part.

Moreover, communication by instant message can be so disorganized that it contributes to feeling overwhelmed, leading to distracted responses and poor follow-through. Some workplaces that rely heavily on IM can have multiple channels going at once. Sometimes it's unclear which channel to use for this topic or that topic. Or you may not remember which channel you or someone else posted something in that you're looking for.

All in all, instant messaging contributes to a general lack of organization of communication interactions.

Additionally, because IMs are challenging to retain, and most likely because of the extremely casual nature of the medium, people may be more likely to type things that could get them into trouble legally, such as inappropriate comments. But just because IMs are hard to track doesn't mean they are ephemeral; the words you type in an IM can absolutely be used against you in a legal situation. Whether or not the IMs involved were actually inappropriate in any way in a particular situation, nevertheless, there are now multiple court cases in which businesses have been compelled by the courts to submit Slack messages as evidence.

Pagefreezer, an archiving software solutions firm, describes the landmark case of Benebone LLC v. Pet Qwerks, in which patent infringement, trade dress (physical appearance) infringement, and unfair competition were being litigated:

"... a court order held that Benebone's Slack messages were discoverable because they were relevant to the eDiscovery requests made by Pet Qwerks.

The court ruled that 'requiring the review and production of Slack messages by Benebone is generally comparable to requiring search and production of emails and is not unduly burdensome or disproportional to the needs of this case—if the requests and searches are appropriately limited and focused.'

This was in response to Benebone's legal team claiming that the plaintiff's Slack account contained approximately 30,000 messages, estimating that it would cost between $110,000 and $255,000 to extract, process, and review those messages.

Based on these cost estimates, the plaintiff argued that searching and producing Slack messages would be an undue burden and not proportional to the needs of the case. The defendants disagreed, filing a motion to compel the plaintiff to produce any Slack messages relevant to the case.

The Magistrate Judge supported the defendants, stating:

'Here, because Benebone uses Slack as part of its internal business communications, there is no real dispute that Benebone's Slack messages are likely to contain relevant information.'"

What this case tells us is that Slack communications are discoverable and will generally be treated in the same manner as emails. This will no doubt apply to instant messages through any channel, not just Slack. So, it is important to avoid the fallacy that the casual nature of an instant-message medium means those messages "don't count" as communication. To both your colleagues and the courts, they do.

Instant messages also tend to be less secure than other means of digital communication. According to Chron.com, instant messages are less secure due to high risk of hacking. For example, there have been two high-profile incidents of Slack being hacked—once with a gaming company called Electronic Arts and the other through Twitter. In both cases, an unwitting employee accidentally granted access to the hackers. And although it is possible for companies to customize their IM security, few actually do it.

Another issue with using instant messaging is that there is often a lack of consistent agreement on how, when, and why to use IM. I, myself, struggled with this in a previous role. I supervised a team at the time, and we were drowning in emails, so we decided to pursue a project-management platform with IM capability. We had several conversations about what types of messages and needs should be handled via email and what types by IM, and we never did reach a consensus. Thus, some people still relied mostly on email, while others switched over to IM. I was loath to implement any type of requirement about how to communicate and when and how to be available, but the lack of that structure created challenges. For example, one woman on the team told me that IM was her preference; however, she almost always had her automatic reply on, notifying me that she was busy or unavailable via IM. So, as her manager, how was I to respect what she had told me was her preference but also be able to communicate with her when I needed to? This is just my experience, but it illustrates a common constraint I hear from many professionals about how hard it is to create mutually acceptable boundaries about the access vs. intrusion that Slack, Teams, and other IM platforms create.

Closely related to the previous point about agreement on how, when, and why to use IM is the downside of immediate access. Yes, getting prompt answers to questions is wonderful sometimes. But on the flip side, IM fosters the assumption that an immediate answer is required, imperative...a given. But that is not always true. Just because we *want* an immediate answer doesn't mean we really need one (don't we want everything immediately these days?). And more importantly, our priorities may not be directly aligned with our recipient's priorities or capabilities.

The most commonly cited downside to IM is that it is a workplace distraction, and that rather than enabling productivity as it claims, it's actually a productivity killer. The critics of platforms like Slack and Teams make compelling arguments to support this point.

In a *Medium* article, software programmer Alicia Liu noted this about Slack:

"By lowering the barrier to initiate communication, the hidden side effect is that Slack has the quiet capacity to exponentially increase communication overhead. Resulting in much more voluminous, lower-quality communication."

And a 2019 *Vox* article offered this compelling piece of data about IMs and productivity:

"Notably, the total amount of time we spend communicating is roughly the same as it was six years ago. That means the addition of workplace chat apps hasn't actually lessened the amount of time we spend communicating."

Lucas Miller, a lecturer at Haas School of Business at Berkeley University and co-founder of productivity consultancy at Stoa Partners, suggests that the problem is less about the platform itself and more about how humans use it. He says:

> "Slack is instant and we get a rewarding hit of dopamine every time we respond to someone or someone reaches out to us to let us know a member of our 'work tribe' needs us. It makes us feel valued and informed, but it also makes us fearful every time an alert comes in that we'll be out of the loop or ill-informed if we don't check a message, even though very few truly need our instant attention."

Thus, the result is workers spend more time checking messages *about* work than actually doing any.

These are sobering arguments regarding the downsides to using instant messaging. And they all add up to what I see as the most concerning problem with IMs as it pertains to communication effectiveness, which is that—in part because it *is* so distracting—people tend to communicate so poorly via IM.

- People don't explain things well enough.
- People make comments with no context.
- People assume you remember something from earlier in the chat.
- People are too abrupt or terse.

The IM platform makes it easy to forget many of the fundamental characteristics of effective communication; namely, clarity, context, and positive tone. These things will just never go away.

In IM, we are relying on the actual words to do the heavy lifting. But that isn't how communication works. *Psychology Today* reports that research by Professor Albert Mehrabian of UCLA found that the impact of communication is determined 38 percent by voice quality, 55 percent by nonverbal communication, and *a mere 7 percent by the words used*. This suggests that when you IM someone, because they can't hear your voice and/or see your facial and body expressions, you are at high risk of them misunderstanding and/or misinterpreting your words. What can you do about this? Well, of course, this is one raison d'etre for emojis. Although I don't recommend using emojis in highly formal written communications, they can be useful in IMs as a way to help communicate intended meaning and emotions. But this is certainly not foolproof. Thus, I also recommend reading your IM very carefully before hitting "send." Ask yourself if there is anything you could add to it to make your meaning more clear.

For example, consider the following exchange between me and a colleague I'll call Regina:

> **Regina:** Did you see the new policy about travel reimbursements?

> **Me:** Yes, I did. Should we share it with the team since you mentioned they had some questions?

> **Regina:** I guess.

Regina's response of "I guess" is fairly vague, and there are lots of ways I could take that. I might assume she didn't really like my suggestion; in fact, worst-case scenario, I could read her response as a bit rude or terse. Or I might wonder if she herself is lacking some clarity about the policy. She could provide more clarity for *me* by remembering that I am lacking other contextual cues, so she needs to provide them for me. What is her emotion here? What other information could she provide that would help me understand what "I guess" means in this conversation?

The following revised response may be more helpful for me.

> **Regina:** Did you see the new policy about travel reimbursements?

> **Me:** Yes, I did. Should we share it with the team since you mentioned they had some questions?

> **Regina:** I guess. Although I wonder if you and I should go over it in detail first to be sure we're on the same page. Then we can share it with the team.

> **Me:** Great idea! I'll book us some time.

This suggestion to take care to provide contextual and emotional cues for your recipient leads me to suggestions for mitigating the other downsides of IM that I've highlighted in this chapter. Although none of these are panaceas, since IM as a tool likely isn't going anywhere, employing these suggestions will make your IM communication much more effective.

In terms of the difficulty in tracking instant messages, there are apps for merging all your instant-messaging apps/platforms into the same place; however, this just means they're all on one dashboard, not that the messages themselves are any more easily organized. So, if you're communicating about something for which you need or want a record, I recommend you use email rather than IM. You know that moment when you send the IM and think, "Hmmm … I wonder if I might need a record of that later"? I'm a big fan of the better-safe-than-sorry approach. So, if you have that thought, even for a second, then grab that IM in a screenshot, or whatever works for you (copy and paste, etc.), and email it to yourself with a subject line that clearly illustrates the topic, then save that email. It's better to have something you don't need than to need something you don't have.

With regard to the issue of getting into legal troubles via IM, the suggestion is likely rather obvious: just don't ever—EVER—type anything even remotely inappropriate, questionable, unethical, etc. If, for even a second, you pause and wonder if it's OK to type something, then the answer is probably NO—do not send whatever it is. That pause is your gut instinct—listen to it! And of course, this doesn't mean that an IM you write will never be used as evidence because, in some cases, it's not that you wrote something inappropriate, but that you wrote something that serves as evidence for some argument. But at least you can try to ensure you aren't in trouble *because of* what you wrote. As a general rule, I recommend avoiding the following:

- Comments of any kind about co-workers. This includes compliments. Sometimes what you think is a compliment, someone else may find offensive. Just don't talk about other people in any way via IM.
- Complaints about your organization or anyone in it.
- Information that your company considers confidential. Because the security of IM is questionable, it's best to use email, phone, or face-to-face communication to discuss sensitive or confidential information.

I also talked about a lack of consistent agreement about how, when, and why to use IM. I'll merge that with the downsides of assuming immediate availability and of IM being a "productivity killer" because I think these issues all go hand-in-hand.

Most experts agree that it is important to craft agreed-upon protocols for using instant messaging, and that these protocols should be communicated over and over again to current and new-hire employees. It would be wise to make these protocols as specific as possible, but also to craft them within a larger conversation about organizational values around time, work expectations, etc.

For example, if you and/or your teammates feel the crush of IM and admit that it is negatively impacting productivity, these protocols could include the rule that colleagues should avoid IM-ing any questions that can wait for a weekly check-in or other regularly scheduled meeting. Co-create parameters about what types of communications are IM-worthy and what types of communications can wait for a meeting, or at least be sent via email instead of IM.

I have a colleague who manages a team, and he shared with me that his team has used this approach and taken it even one step further, agreeing that email subject lines must contain a deadline. He told me his team has found this to be incredibly helpful as it has decreased the number of IMs they receive, and it has allowed them to quickly prioritize emails from one another.

This example also demonstrates that, even if your organization as a whole does not craft such protocols, you could take the reins and request your team or department works together to create them.

Experts also suggest training HR liaisons in how to effectively deal with complaints and concerns about instant messages. Given that new complications could continue to arise with this medium, it would be fruitful for HR professionals to be adept at navigating sticky situations that may arise.

In terms of the expectation for immediate responses, let's talk first about your expectation of others' responses. My recommendation is to temper your expectations in your own communication. First, pay attention to the recipient's auto-reply message. If it says they aren't available right now, wait to send the IM or at least let them know you don't need an immediate response (providing an actual deadline would be even more helpful). My second recommendation is to temper your expectations mentally. In our evermore instant-gratification culture, it can be easy to trick ourselves into thinking we have to have this thing or that thing right now. But learn to table things and move on. I bet you still do this at home, don't you? For example, if you're waiting to fold laundry, you don't sit in front of the dryer and watch the wet clothes dry. You put them in, hit start, then go do something else until they're dry. Then, if you're like me, you leave them there for hours until they wrinkle! But I think you get my point, which is to move on to another task until you receive the answer to the question you sent.

It is also incumbent upon you to temper others' expectations. Be sure if you can't reply right away that you do have an appropriate status set that communicates your unavailability to others. Next, be sure that you actually respond at some point. As I mentioned earlier, the number of instant messages and other digital communications we receive every day can feel overwhelming, leading to a lack of follow-through on our part. One trick I use is to go old-school. I keep a pad of paper on my desk and, if I don't respond to someone right away, I jot their name down on my pad, crossing it off only after I have responded. But then again, I still use an old-school, handwritten to-do list, so this suggestion may feel too antiquated for you; if so, find something that feels sustainable for you to help you with follow-through. Although I don't subscribe to the notion that we must reply immediately to every single message (especially if you've set your status as "unavailable" or the like), I do suggest that you ensure proper follow-through with everyone. Human perception being what it is, you must keep in mind that others don't tend to begin with the empathetic thought, "Oh, Ali is probably just overwhelmed and that's why I haven't heard back from her." Most people will think some version of, "What's going on? Why hasn't she responded to me?"

Finally, I recommend using an integrated approach to workplace communications. Work to minimize reliance on instant messages. Create a culture wherein people feel the positive benefits of a quick in-person conversation, Zoom meeting, or phone call. For organizations in which most or all employees are remote, there are many interesting alternatives now popping up, such as Discord, which is a remote co-working space. It's essentially a virtual open room in which one person can hang out and work in case someone else may "pop in" with a quick question—the virtual equivalent of working with your door open. Platforms like these will likely continue to spring up, offering organizations options for decreasing reliance on instant messages.

All in all, I hope the fundamental message of this chapter is clear: stop treating instant messages as if they "don't count" as your communication. They do. It's worth your time to work a little harder to make your IM communication reflect the professional communication brand you want to portray.

Chapter 5

MISTAKE #4: THINKING YOUR TONE DOESN'T MATTER BECAUSE PEOPLE KNOW YOU MEAN WELL

B e honest. Have you ever sent a digital message that you knew had a potentially negative tone, but you sent it anyway? Perhaps you were, indeed, angry. Or perhaps you were just in a hurry and fired something off quickly without giving it much thought. How did the recipient react to your message? Perhaps they let you know your tone didn't land well.

Or perhaps it didn't land well, but they never told you, choosing instead (however subconsciously) to trust you a little bit less moving forward.

I titled the mistake in this chapter the way I did because I've had people tell me that they are aware that some of their emails land in ways that sound terse, snarky, rude, or angry, but they were unconcerned because, as they say, their co-workers "know them well enough" to know they didn't mean anything negative.

But do they? Are you 100 percent sure?

I worked with a woman—I'll call her Mickey—who was practically infamous for the fact that even though she was incredibly kind in person, her emails were egregiously terse, bordering on rude most of the time.

For example, I once emailed Mickey with a question and received this response:

> **Me:** Hi, Mickey. Hope you had a great weekend! Quick question for you. Would you like to be included in the meetings Leah and I will be holding about revising the onboarding process, or would you prefer she just apprises you of the changes we make?

> **Mickey:** I already told her no.

Ouch. It may be that Mickey is simply trying to be concise, which I appreciate. However, there is a difference between being concise and being rude; her response here borders on the latter, not to mention unclear, since I asked her an either/or question.

And this was typical of Mickey's responses. She seemed to almost get a kick out of it, like it was a game to see how abrupt her emails could read while she, herself, was so kind and funny in person. But I'll tell you, the recipients of her emails didn't find it nearly as funny as she did. Multiple people complained to me about her tone, and one colleague even told me that she would prefer not to even communicate with Mickey by email because Mickey's tone so often made her feel ill at ease.

I've mentioned this before, but it bears repeating here: in today's litigious and divisive world, most people will not go to the trouble of telling you if your tone comes across negatively. The risk is just too high for most people; we have built a culture of so much division when differing opinions arise that many people nowadays choose to say nothing rather than risk starting a conflict. So, people will likely not tell you that your digital communications contain a tone they find off-putting; instead, they'll simply adjust how they interact with you, and likely how they talk about you to other people. Brené Brown, in conducting research for her book *Dare to Lead*, found that over half of the senior executives she interviewed noted that their organizational cultures nowadays are infused with a cultural norm of "nice and polite," meaning people go out of their way to avoid tough conversations or any type of critical feedback to others. But this doesn't mean those people are unaffected by poor behavior; on the contrary, they are increasingly likely to engage in problematic behavior like passive-aggression, talking behind your back, and what Brené calls the "dirty yes" (saying "yes" to your face but "no" behind your back).

Remember that this book is about your computer-side manner, the way you present yourself to others in all your communications—digital and face-to-face. If you're interested in minimizing (or even eradicating) this type of toxic politeness and having confidence that your communications aren't working against you, then it's incumbent upon you, *regardless of the medium or context*, to remember this maxim:

The tone of your digital communications is equally as important as the words you use.

Of course, this creates a problem for digital communications because tone is difficult to convey. Although, I think it could be safely argued that digital-communication tone is kind of like respect or oxygen—you may not necessarily notice it when it's positive, but you can certainly identify it when it's not. When someone uses a tone that is off-putting, terse, hostile, etc., you recognize it immediately. But this points directly to another compounding problem, which is that tone is so subjective. While I may not have intended any negative tone when I wrote my message, that doesn't necessarily mean it didn't come across that way to my reader.

A review of literature conducted by Kris Byron reveals that readers of emails tend to use schema (a relatively stable mental framework regarding what one finds typical or usual in a situation as defined by our previous experiences) to filter perceptions of emails, resulting in typically reading emails either more negatively (at worst) or more neutrally (at best) than they were intended. The latter may sound promising—for example, if you sent an email with a negative tone unwittingly—however, the research also demonstrates that emails with positive intent or tone tend to be read more neutrally than intended more often than emails with negative intent or tone.

This is because, as I indicated in Chapter 4, so much of our communication relies on nonverbal cues. There are some options in digital communication to supplement the written word with written cues (emojis, italics, etc.) that are intended to serve as nonverbal cues, but they don't quite do the trick.

One problem is that there is no universally accepted way to communicate emotions in written digital communication. For example, using italics to emphasize something is neither a requirement nor a universally utilized practice. Some organizations even suggest avoiding things like italics, emojis, and caps because they tend to make a message appear less formal.

This is compounded by the fact that words alone just don't cut it when it comes to communicating emotions to the reader. If we describe the fact that we are not feeling a negative emotion in a message, it may do little or nothing to actually communicate that argument. If I type, "I'm not at all angry," somehow my recipient is still likely to question whether I am—even though I just said I'm not.

"A rude communication makes you think less of a person, regardless of your relationship with them. Even when you're dealing with someone you have a professional relationship with, in that moment it becomes personal. It feels like getting stung by a bee. The technology means you have to work harder to make yourself heard. It takes so little—sometimes just one wrong word—to shut down communication."

~Becky Traweek, CEO, Girl Scouts of Greater Mississippi

And research has demonstrated that, left to their own devices (I suppose, in this case, both metaphorical and literal devices), most people are not very good at correctly interpreting emotion even when the author actively tries to convey that emotion. According to a *Fast Company* article, participants in a 2005 research study were only able to correctly interpret an email sender's intended emotion about 56 percent of the time—that's not much better than the percentage of correct interpretation by sheer chance. Yet the percentage of correct interpretation of emotion rose to 73 percent when the same messages were sent via voice message—illuminating once again that audio cues are critical for the correct interpretation of emotion.

The same *Fast Company* article notes:

"Now let's look at such misunderstandings through the lens of the message recipient. It's well-documented among psychologists that when people lack information, they tend to rely on stereotypes to fill in the gaps. In the case of emails and other digital messages, the missing information tends to be a full appreciation of the sender's personality. That's why it's usually clear when a friend or loved one is joking in a note or text, but not always clear that a remote colleague is doing the same."

There is also something called the negativity effect, which says that in the absence of information (such as spoken words or body language in this case), readers will mistake ambiguity for negativity, leading to a more negative reading of the sender's message than the sender likely intended.

The bottom line is that it's quite difficult to accurately portray emotions in an email, making it difficult, in turn, to accurately portray the intent of the message.

This may lead you to ask, "OK, Ali, but what about books? Books succeed in communicating emotions with words quite successfully." And this is a great point! However, consider how realistic it is to write with a book-worthy creative flourish when we communicate in professional situations. Imagine, for example, if you were to write an email to a colleague who has yet to provide you with the information you requested by the agreed-upon deadline. If you were inclined to use a creative-writing approach, your email might look something like this:

> Dearest Humphrey,
>
> Alas, January 5th has come and gone, but with nary an email from you containing the data we amicably agreed you would provide by that date. Imagine my chagrin upon checking my email this morning, hoping against hope to have received your data, only to have my illusions so fervently dashed upon realizing no such email had been received. Oh, Humphrey, dost thou know how readily I must have the data of which we spoke? It provides me no joy, mind

you, to bring this to your attention; on the contrary, I am despondent at the prospect of causing you any grief due to your having caused me as much.

But fear not, dear Humphrey, for I trust that this email will remind you to most hurriedly—and yet, of course, accurately—provide me with the data that will no doubt alight my heart with joy.

Most sincerely yours,
Martha

Even though your colleague would likely think you've flipped your lid—and this letter is admittedly a bit flowery for today's writers—you simply don't have time to write this way in a professional setting. Not to mention, doing so would put a serious damper on your ability to employ my previous chapter's suggestion to be concise!

All this information about how difficult it is to successfully convey a positive tone is compounded even more by the fact that most people, when reading emails and other digital communications, are likely half-reading. Due to distractions, attempts at multi-tasking (which I'll discuss in the next chapter), or time constraints, most people don't give digital communications their full attention, which increases the likelihood of misreading words AND tone.

So, how *do* you ensure you are avoiding a negative tone and, even better, ensuring a positive one when you send digital communications?

First, there is the question of what the tone should be. You don't necessarily need to strike the same tone with everyone you communicate with; for example, some digital communications can have a more casual tone while some require a more formal tone. And it's perfectly acceptable for some to have a more serious tone while others carry a more ebullient one. But irrespective of those things, all your digital communications should have a *positive* tone—that is, respectful of the recipient.

This doesn't mean all your digital communications must be happy, agreeable, etc. It's perfectly acceptable to express concern, dissent, confusion, or the like via email or IM (it is not acceptable to handle conflict via digital communications, but we'll tackle that in a later chapter). But you should always ensure that your tone takes into consideration the best possible delivery of your concerns, fears, etc. so that they land on the reader in a way that feels collaborative, not adversarial. Remember: people are more likely to read your tone as more negatively than you mean it. So, it's up to you to do the work to try to ensure that doesn't happen. As I elucidated in Chapter 3, the onus is always on you, the communicator, not your recipient.

Of course, you cannot fully control the other person's reaction. Perhaps the recipient is having a horrible day or is already upset at you for something else—these things would certainly color their perspective of your message.

So, how do you work to ensure that your tone comes across as positively as possible to help ensure your recipient is relying less on "filling in the gaps" in your words? Keep the following suggestions in mind **every time** you write a digital communication.

Use Positive Language Rather Than Negative

Be careful to phrase your message in a positive light by using positive words rather than negative ones. For example, if you were writing a colleague about a report that you felt wasn't quite up to par yet, rather than saying, "This report still needs a lot of work," say "Great work on the report so far. Are you open to my sharing some suggestions to ensure it meets the goals the VP outlined?"

Use Provisional Language Rather Than Certain Language

My second strategy for ensuring a positive tone is to use what's called provisional language rather than certain language. These are terms from a communication framework called Gibb categories, which are pretty widely known among those who study interpersonal communication, but maybe less so outside that field. Certainty and provisionalism are concepts that exist on opposite ends of a spectrum. When we exhibit certainty, we're convinced that we are right. Period. And that no amount of additional information will change that fact; therefore, we are uninterested in receiving any. Certainty is actually what's known as a disconfirming behavior; when you display it, you demonstrate a lack of regard for others and their ideas. Provisionalism, on the other hand, is a lens characterized by listening with an open mind and being open to others' opinions. Being provisional doesn't mean you might not have strong opinions; it just means that you acknowledge the possibility that you might not be right, or that others' opinions have merit.

So, how does this manifest in digital writing? Certainty often manifests in language that's more concrete or absolute. Words like *can't, won't, never, always,* or *must* demonstrate certainty. Whereas words like *perhaps, might,* or *possibly* communicate provisionalism.

For example, you might be tempted to write something like this:

> **The only way to get everyone on the same page is to make a new policy.**

But that would communicate certainty; you're suggesting that your way is the only way. That will not convey a positive tone.

Instead, use provisional language that communicates openness to another perspective. Something like:

> **I have some ideas, but I'd love to hear your suggestions for possible next steps.**

Notice that, by asking the other person's perspective, I suggested there's more than one way forward. Notice, also, that I didn't even ask, "What's your opinion of how we might get everyone on the same page?" because even **that** suggests that getting everyone on the same page is the correct course of action, and it may not be. Maybe that's not the most logical answer to the issue. To be truly provisional, you must use language that demonstrates openness to alternative points of view and courses of action. Doing so will go a long way toward creating a positive tone.

Be Relational

Have you ever received an email or text from someone that contained a missive or request with no greeting of any kind? Perhaps you opened the email to read the following:

> *I need you to find out if the venue charges for parking.*

Even if that was worded more congenially, perhaps, "Can you find out if the venue charges for parking?" it may still have felt a little abrupt to you.

Emails, texts, and even IMs to colleagues should generally contain some element of relationship-establishing and maintaining. This is not your spouse, your brother, or your roommate; this is a professional colleague. Cement both your reputation as an effective communicator and your positive relationship with that person by including a bit of collegial talk.

If you were physically in your office, you would likely never walk into a colleague's office and abruptly say, "I need to request a meeting" or "Have you had time to look at the analysis yet?" without first offering some kind of greeting. If we did that, we would probably have some struggles with our professional relationships. Instead, we typically say things like, "Good morning, Shay, how are you? Did you have a nice weekend?" and we have some friendly banter. Then we move into the reason for coming to her office. By the same token, you wouldn't call a professional contact and blurt out, "Did you review the client agreement I sent?" the second they pick up the phone. Yet…we sometimes do these things via email! I've received many an email that demonstrated the written equivalent of these examples. So, be sure to begin with a warm opener when emailing your professional contacts. Of course, this doesn't mean launching into a three-paragraph story about the difficult time you're having as a new empty nester (hypothetically speaking)! Remember, conciseness is still the name of the game. But even a simple, "Greetings, Terry, happy Monday!" can go a long way toward making your tone more friendly.

And in the same manner, end your communications with a thank you at the very least. Ending a digital communication to a colleague with no closing is akin to talking on the phone with them and hanging up on them abruptly. You may think I'm being overly cautious—well, maybe I am…but wouldn't you rather err on the side of caution when it comes to building strong professional relationships?

Read the Message Out Loud

You'd be surprised how different your written communications can sound when you read them aloud vs. only in your head. When we read silently, we are tempted (especially if we are feeling rushed) to "speed read," which most of us aren't skilled at, meaning we are likely to skip words and read what we think we wrote rather than what we actually wrote.

Plus, if you read aloud you're more likely to hear the tone of the actual words you typed, not the intention behind your words. That intention is likely to shape your perception of them when you read silently, but reading them out loud will increase the likelihood that you hear them how your recipient will read them. I have revised many digital communications after reading them out loud! I urge you to do the same.

Pick Up the Phone!

Or walk into their office. Or use Zoom. But you get the point: rely more often on communication that includes audio and, when possible, visual cues. We over-rely on email and IM these days because we think it's faster. But ask yourself if it really is faster when we so frequently spend time dealing with relational or personnel issues that arise due to negative reactions to **how** something was said (not to mention the time spent correcting poorly written content).

These tips should help ensure your tone lands as positively as possible. Remember that this is all in service of creating and protecting your brand as an excellent communicator (and, by extension, a valuable employee and colleague).

To that end, I'll leave you with one last thought in this chapter. Maybe you don't think your tone has ever been off-putting. But are you sure? Remember that I mentioned earlier that, nowadays, most people will never tell you if you've sent digital communications with a tone that didn't land well with them, but that doesn't mean it hasn't happened.

Because of what I do for a living, I'm in the unique position of being on the receiving end of countless stories that professionals have told me about their coworkers' communication skills that they either can't or won't share with their coworkers. For example, I was talking with a gentleman named Shane, who is the chief information officer (CIO) of a local production company. Shane told me this story about a gentleman—let's call him Ken—with whom he worked and who had problematic communication skills. In particular, Ken tended to communicate very rudely via email, and his colleagues found it upsetting and considered him "aggressive." Despite receiving coaching for his tone, he continued to send emails and IMs that were rude, terse, and overly direct. Consequently, Ken was passed over multiple times for possible promotions and raises. Shane said that it would have been entirely possible that Ken had become the CIO rather than him, had his communication not been received so poorly (and had he not neglected as he did to make the recommended improvements to his communication).

Perhaps you read this story and think, well, maybe Ken didn't really want to move up. Perhaps. But Shane also shared with me that Ken's communication is so poor, and he has been reprimanded so many times, that not only has he failed to move upward in the company, but he has also consistently been ranked the lowest on his team, which means he has also been passed over several times for pay increases. I doubt the latter was part of his career plan.

I tell you this story to drive home the point that you must work hard to ensure your communications are received positively—you truly must **proactively** think about your tone and go out of your way to ensure it lands as positively as possible since, as we just learned, in the absence of vocal or nonverbal cues, people will tend to assume the worst.

I also tell you this story to drive home the point I started the chapter with: people who communicate with a poor tone tend to have the attitude that "people know me better than that." Believe it or not, my colleague Shane told me that Ken said a version of that exact phrase to him; Ken said to him one day, "I don't get it. People know me. Why can't they just assume I mean well?" I feel deep empathy for Ken in his asking that question. I get it. But, unfortunately, the fairly simple answer to Ken's question is that it's just not human nature. The way you are received by your colleagues is impacted greatly by **each** communicative interaction you have with them—and some might even argue it is always impacted by the most recent interaction you've had with them.

Let me offer a comparison that may hit home. If you think people are supposed to just know you mean well, and thus always assume positive intent, think about this: how many times has your significant other said to you, "Are you mad at me?" or "What's bugging you?" when absolutely nothing was wrong? How many times have YOU said the same to them? **If you two don't know each other well enough to be 100 percent certain of positive intent all the time, why would you assume your colleagues do?**

Friedrich Nietzsche offered, "We often contradict an opinion for no other reason than that we do not like the tone in which it is expressed." Don't let your digital tone be the reason your voice isn't heard.

Chapter 6

MISTAKE #5: THINKING IT'S OK THAT YOU'RE NOT MENTALLY PRESENT IN A ZOOM MEETING BECAUSE YOU'RE GOOD AT MULTITASKING

When I was in academic leadership, I was in a Zoom meeting with a team I supervised and with an assistant dean in our department. The assistant dean, Debra, had just told my team that we were going to hit pause on one aspect of a plan we had been creating, but move ahead with the rest of the plan. She explained why, then went around the virtual room to ask each person directly whether they had any questions or concerns. When she got to Connor, which was at least five people later, it was clear he had not been paying attention, and when she asked if he had any questions, he stammered, "Oh … um … I guess … just …" and then he proceeded to ask if there were any updates about the exact phase of the plan she just spent five minutes explaining that we were holding off on. It made him look incompetent in front of everyone, and it created a lack of trust and credibility in him in her eyes. (Names have been changed.)

I bet this faux pas resonates with a lot of people. Not even I will feign total innocence here. I TEACH communication skills and I've … ahem … attended to other tasks during a Zoom meeting or two.

We're all overwhelmed these days. We all have too much to do. And we think if we can *just do this one other thing* during the meeting, we'll be so much less stressed.

But here's the thing. We won't be. Research reveals a few important things about multitasking.

First, you're **not** good at it. You're not even capable of it. No one is.

No matter how hard you try to convince yourself, the whole concept of multitasking is a myth. The brain is simply not capable of attending to two cognitively complex actions at the same time. Notice I said *complex actions*—things like listening, reading, writing, and talking. These take more cognitive energy than, say, doodling, tapping your foot, or twirling your hair.

What does happen is what's called taskswitching. So, we, in effect, are not actually engaging in two tasks at once, but rather switching back and forth between two or more tasks quickly.

Although some researchers do believe it is possible that the brain could be trained to taskswitch more effectively, even that's debated for now. What researchers **do** agree on is that, at least currently, as John Medina says in his book, *Brain Rules*, our brains are "biologically incapable of processing attention-rich inputs simultaneously."

In other words, although we fool ourselves into thinking we're multitasking because we're technically doing more than one task, we aren't doing any of them very well, and we're certainly not creating any neural connections—that is, in layperson's terms, we are pretty much incapable of effectively analyzing, assessing, evaluating, remembering, or learning in those moments when we think we're multitasking.

> "You can have a really negative outcome when someone is not paying attention and they miss what they're supposed to do, which creates a missed deliverable for the client or a misunderstanding over who's doing what. And then it falls back on whoever's most responsible to get the job done. In general, it's deeper than a tangible 'this is what might happen.' It starts to erode the ability for members to work together, create trust between each other, and build better work relationships. Work gets problematic not usually over the work, but over the people. When you have this dynamic where some people are [present] and some people are not, or you can tell some people are multitasking or not listening, it can create resentments and affect the team dynamic."
> ~ Greg Norton, National Practice Leader,
> Marsh McLennan

The second important thing to understand about multi-tasking is that we do it (for the most part) because we *think* if we can just knock one more thing off our plate, we'll be less stressed. But this is not true. Research reveals that multitasking adds to our stress levels by increasing cortisol and adrenaline. Additionally, it weakens memory and creativity, and temporarily decreases your IQ while you're doing it!

Before I move to the third important thing to understand about multitasking, I'll ask you to guess something. No Googling! What do you think the average human attention span is?

I ask this because I suggest that the reason we multitask isn't always because we're trying to accomplish things. Sometimes we do it because we rationalize multitasking by telling ourselves that we can't help it because (please imagine me using facetious air quotes here) "humans have shorter attention spans nowadays." I'm using those air quotes (can you call them air quotes if they're written?) because people say this to me all the time as an excuse for multitasking.

But it turns out that my question about the average human attention span was a bit of a trick question because the whole notion of attention span is a myth. Maybe you've even heard the one about humans now having the same attention span as your average goldfish.

The truth is that attention is selective. Period.

Dr. Gemma Briggs, a psychologist who studies attention at the Open University near London, notes that the whole notion of an "average attention span" is a myth. Attention is task dependent. And it has everything to do with the extent to which a person is motivated to selectively attend to something. So, if something interests you, it will keep your attention; if it doesn't, it won't. If you see a car crash (real or proverbial), you don't lose interest just because you've been watching for twelve seconds.

By the way, as a quick and humorous side note, Simon Maybin of the BBC World Service found an expert on fish behavior (yep, that's right, a fish-behavior expert) who says goldfish are actually quite capable of memory and learning and do not, in fact, have short attention spans either!

It is certainly true that, in today's digitally polluted world, more things are competing for our selective attention. But attention *is* a choice. And for you to be—and be viewed as—a more effective communicator, focusing your attention is a choice you should make. When we don't choose focused attention, we fail to remain present in Zoom meetings or on phone calls. We send emails, texts, and IMs that are unclear, confusing, or lack proper tone. We make stupid, embarrassing, or even costly communication mistakes. In short, we are not very good communicators.

Does simply choosing to focus your attention sound easier said than done? Maybe. But, like the other myths and strategies in this book, this is about making a proactive choice to communicate in a way that reflects the professional brand you want to build. Not to mention that the research on the brain definitively illustrates that multitasking greatly diminishes your capacity to think critically and process information accurately while you are engaging in it, meaning that the likelihood of your learning or remembering anything you hear while you're multitasking is very slim.

Now, the good news! You absolutely CAN choose to focus on particular things (assuming average cognitive ability, that is; not wanting to focus your attention and not being able to aren't the same thing). And you can do things to help focus your attention more purposefully to avoid the aforementioned negative outcomes.

The first, most obvious, and easiest thing you can do to focus your attention more purposefully is to turn off the tools, alerts, devices, etc. that compete for your attention during meetings. It's as simple as that. I don't have any hacks or strategies other than to make the choice to turn them off and stick with it.

But let's dig deeper than that and examine strategies you can engage to help you develop longer and stronger attention spans. Your attention span is, to put it simply, just like a muscle. And if you haven't been exercising it, it likely has become weaker. But just like a physical muscle in your body, the fact that it may be weaker does not mean you can't build it up again. If you want bigger biceps, that takes work. The same is true for a longer attention span. There are some strategies you can engage to help build your attention-span muscle.

First, keep to-do lists. I am a big fan of to-do lists. I have multiple lists; some are for smaller, random items like, "sharpen knives, ask neighbor where she got the red chair on her deck, and hang pictures in guest bedroom" (Andrew Cohen of Brainscape, a successful study app, calls these "ticky-tacky items"). And I have some lists for larger, everyday items such as grocery lists and work-related to-do items.

The second suggestion to help build your attention span is to have a dedicated way to keep "not now" lists. These are lists of those random items that pop into your head while you're trying to focus on something else—like a Zoom meeting, for example. If you have a dedicated place to capture these items when they come up, you eliminate the feeling that they have to get done right then because capturing them means you won't forget them. And you must resist the urge to think "Oh, this will only take a sec" because … well … whom are we kidding? It always takes longer than you think it will, and there's always another rabbit hole to go down. So, get into the habit of capturing those pop-up items on your "not now" list and leave them there until you can give them your full attention.

The third tip for building your attention-span muscle is to read. Specifically, you should read longer books and books that are more difficult. This doesn't mean you necessarily have to bite the bullet and finally read *War and Peace* (though if you want to, don't let me stand in the way!). But it does mean you should opt for books that challenge you—only you can decide where that bar is set. But the challenge is what's important because we have become a culture of short reads—quick articles, bulleted lists, and even sometimes just headlines. And again, not flexing your attention-span muscle by reading longer items simply trains your brain to be less effective at doing it. So, if you want to increase your attention span, you'll need to read longer and more complicated content. If this is new to you, it will take some time to do well, but resist the temptation to think it's just not possible. It is! Think back to the muscle analogy. If you're trying to lose 30 pounds, you can't do it all in one day. It's about making healthy choices every day and losing a little bit each day. Improving your ability to read and expanding your attention span are no different. You may wish to visit *www.bookriot.com* for some tips on how to read with intentionality and avoid skimming.

Not only will this new practice increase your attention span, but it will also expand your vocabulary and make you a more interesting person!

The next tip for improving your attention is to exercise. Experts note that exercise is valuable in teaching us to ignore distractions and persevere through difficult moments. Although fitness is highly important to me, I understand that not everyone shares that view. A friend of mine was told by her doctor that she needed to exercise to help her health. I thought I could find a way to help her view exercise as fun, so I asked her what type of activity she enjoyed doing, to which she replied, "I enjoy *not* exercising." So, I get it! Fitness isn't everyone's cup of tea. But if you can find some type of physical activity to do for at least thirty minutes a day, you will increase your ability to concentrate, not to mention a whole host of other physical and mental health benefits.

The fifth tip for improving your ability to focus is to practice active listening. Listening attentively to others is not only critical in meetings, especially Zoom meetings, but also in all areas of life. When we are engaged in interactions with others, attentive listening is critical to be a good communicator—and, frankly, a good colleague, partner, friend, etc. Yet, if you think about it, it is one of the times we are likely the worst at focusing our attention. Think of the people you've known in your life who have made you feel truly heard, valued, supported, and understood. I guarantee you that, as you look back now, you'll realize it's because that person is an excellent listener. We just cannot be good communicators or good personal or professional partners without being attentive listeners. So, honing your listening skills will, first and foremost, have the important impact of making you a stronger communicator, but it also has the bonus of helping improve your overall concentration.

This last tip is so obvious (and meta?) that it may seem tongue-in-cheek, but it's not. In fact, it's supported by many experts in this area. If you want to get better at focusing your attention, you have to ... well ... practice focusing your attention. Make the active choice to focus on one thing at a time anytime you're communicating digitally. And make the active choice to do that for longer and longer periods. Yes, this will take some practice, but it is as simple as a conscious choice—nothing more or less. When you feel the pull of a different task when you're in a meeting, talk positively to yourself about what you've learned in this chapter regarding the value of being truly present. Then make the choice to stay that way.

If you're not sure how exactly to practice focusing your attention, try these tricks, which were reported in an *Inc.* article and were originally written by Theron Q. Dumont in his book, *The Power of Concentration*, in 1918.

- Sit still in a chair and do nothing else for five minutes.
- Concentrate on slowly opening and closing your fists for five minutes.
- Follow the second hand of a clock for five minutes.

Apparently, five minutes was a really big thing for Mr. Dumont. But most mindfulness gurus will also tell you to do any mindfulness exercise for at least five minutes. I haven't been able to find any specific research on why five minutes is always the suggestion, but I assume that they are attempting to make it as easy as possible, with the assumption that most people have at least five minutes a day to devote to making their lives better. And I agree! Though, many experts note that even *one* minute a day of meditation or focused-concentration exercise is enough to have powerful positive benefits!

When you choose to focus your attention in these ways, you will improve your computer-side manner, which increases the likelihood that others will view you as an effective communicator—and increases the likelihood that they will want to pay more attention to you in return! Now we're talking about *really* connecting with people when we communicate—and that just feels so much better!

So remember: it's a *choice* to be present. It's not an accident not to be.

Chapter 7

MISTAKES #6 & #7: THINKING YOU DON'T HAVE TIME TO EDIT AND THINKING SHORT COMMUNICATIONS DON'T NEED TO BE EDITED

Although in the introduction to this book, I said I would be explaining one mistake per chapter, the two communication mistakes referenced in the title of this chapter are so closely related (and yet distinct enough to be considered separate), that I want to discuss them in tandem.

Ask yourself how many times you've sent a text, email, or IM that contained an error that you had to send a follow-up communication to correct or clear up. If we each had a way to go back and count, I'd bet most of us would count hundreds, if not thousands, of these moments over the course of our professional lives. Some of us might count dozens this week!

I'll share one that haunts me to this day. About eighteen years ago, just after I had completed my Ph.D., I launched a freelance editing business. I truly enjoy editing other people's work because it allows me to serve others while utilizing my own strengths. I was so excited. I had made numerous contacts in the higher-education world by then, so I decided to focus on academic clientele since I knew the ins and outs of being published in journals and academic texts. I thought it would be a good idea to send a letter to 200 or so of my professional contacts, letting them know about my new endeavor (this was before the days of mass email marketing, and I wanted a personal touch since I legitimately knew all of these people). In this letter, I bragged about my knowledge of academic publishing as well as my "eagle eye." I also included a few business cards for my new business, which I had named Allison Editorial. About a week after I sent these letters out, I received an email from a former professor whom, by then, I considered a trusted colleague. In his email, he congratulated me on the new endeavor…and then he dropped the bomb that continues to resonate in my head all these years later. He told me that my business name was misspelled on my business card. My business cards said "Allison Editoral."

At first, I thought, "Surely, he's mistaken. That can't be true." But I went to look at my business cards (apparently for the first time?), and, sure enough, there it was: Editoral. Oh no. I was mortified. Reeling with embarrassment and dismay, I wanted to crawl into a hole and never come out. How had this happened?

The answer, of course, was that in my excitement about the idea of getting my fancy new business cards and sending out this letter (which I thought was sure to result in more business than I could handle), I simply had not taken the time to proofread my business cards.

What do you think happened next? I'll tell you: nothing. Absolutely nothing. I never got a single job from anyone on that contact list. And rightly so. Would *you* hire an editor who can't correctly spell "editorial?" I wouldn't.

I'm happy to report that, despite this very rocky and embarrassing launch, I did go on to have a successful editing business for about a decade. And, if anything, that mistake was a blessing because it taught me the very principle on which this chapter is founded: you MUST edit your words. Always. Sometimes the lessons that stick with us the most are the ones that were the hardest and most painful to learn.

But I'm writing this so that you can learn from my lesson! Well, that is, if you haven't already gone through at least one (or several) of these incidents yourself. I hope you haven't, but whether you have or haven't, this chapter will offer you the sound rationale for always editing your communications (regardless of length!) and some strategies for doing so efficiently.

As I said, I assume that if you're reading this book, you have had at least one, if not several, of these types of moments. Those moments when you sent something to someone and then realized (on your own or as a result of that person's response) that you inadvertently made a mistake that made your communication confusing, incorrect, awkward, rude, or the like.

Think back to those moments. How did you feel when it happened? Embarrassed? Worried? Ashamed? Silly? Unworthy? Just plain dumb? (Again, I've been there, too, so no judgment!)

You may have had more of those moments than you realize, because if they made you feel any of those negative feelings, rather than learn from them and have them burned on your brain like mine was, you may have rationalized them away. MIT neuroscientist Tali Sharot researched what motivates people to change, and she and her team found that we dislike bad news about ourselves so much that we are masters at rationalizing it away. Negative information makes us feel bad about ourselves, so we simply block it out and gravitate toward positive views of ourselves and our behaviors instead.

It's also entirely possible that you have made those kinds of mistakes and the recipient just never told you. Let that sink in for a moment. How many times have you sent something that would—had you known about it—embarrass you or misrepresent the quality, intention, or time spent on your work? Chances are it has happened because, as I've mentioned in previous chapters, especially in today's divisive and litigious world, people are less likely than ever to offer you honest feedback (especially unsolicited). But that doesn't mean their perception of you is positive, or even neutral, if you sent something that should have been edited more effectively.

By this point, I hope I've convinced you that you should spend more time editing your communications. But you may still be thinking, "Yeah, but that's only true if it's something longer, complex, or really important. Right???"

In short, no. You should edit all your communications, regardless of length or complexity. Just because the communication itself may be short doesn't necessarily mean incorrect, confusing, or poorly written verbiage has any less of an impact. Let me offer you two examples.

A colleague of mine I'll call Keith sent a one-sentence email that caused a great deal of confusion and wasted time for the people who received it. Keith manages a team of about a dozen IT developers. One day they were experiencing a system issue, which Keith had set out to rectify. He sent the following email to his team:

"The system is not up and running."

What he meant to write was, "The system is **now** up and running." An important distinction in this case. Keith waited and waited for other people to begin the tasks that had been put on pause due to the system issue, but no one did anything because, of course, they thought the system was still down. He reached out to the team with what he admits was an impatiently worded email inquiring as to where everyone was and why no one was doing their respective tasks. It was only then that he realized the error as people explained their response (or lack thereof) due to what he had actually written.

The result was a good deal of wasted time as Keith waited for people (in a business where an hour is an **eternity**) to do their jobs. And he had some relational repair to do because his snarky email didn't sit well with some of the staff who, of course, due to his typo, had no idea they were able to move forward with their tasks.

I'll share another example with you. I recently received a request to connect with a woman on LinkedIn. She sent me the following message (verbatim except for the company name):

> "Hey, I came across your profile while searching for leaders in Technology, Information, and the Internet. Reaching out to connect and discuss possible business development.
>
> This is (your name) from ABC Company; We are an expert team with 15+ years of experience combined. Let's Connect"

There are a few issues with this message that perhaps only someone like me would notice; for example, the inappropriately casual greeting from someone I've never met, the punctuation and capitalization errors, and the fact that there is no explanation of what type of company she represents. However, surely any person would notice the glaring mistake where the woman did not insert her own name in the template message she was using. It actually came to me with "This is (your name)" in the message. Yikes. I'm guessing personalized service is not their specialty. Needless to say, I did not respond to her.

We're all inundated with messages like these all the time. **Now more than ever it matters whether you write clearly, because people look for *any* excuse to ignore or dismiss your communication.**

I'd like to offer one more example to illustrate why it is critical to edit even short communications. A few years ago, I was composing an email to the VP of Human Resources for the organization I worked for at the time. She had done me a favor, and I was crafting a quick response to thank her. I wrote the six-word email—so short it couldn't possibly need editing! Right? Wrong. And thank goodness I took the time to edit.

Here's what I meant to write:

"Thank you so much. You're awesome!"

Here's what I had actually written:

"Thank you so much. You're awful!"

I don't know about you, but I don't think that's the type of thing one generally wants to send to the VP of Human Resources. Luckily, I had learned from my business-card fiasco and followed my own advice to edit even the shortest communications, so I caught it. But I never forgot it. (Better me than her!)

I've already covered in previous chapters the multitudes of ways poorly written (unclear, confusing, erroneous, etc.) communications negatively affect your professional reputation and possibly your relationships. Each of these examples illustrates that impact. And again, when you know about it, it's embarrassing. But there are likely countless examples you never got feedback on. How did those impact your work? Your relationships? Your professional reputation?

So, the lesson here is to edit all your communications regardless of length or complexity.

I often hear some common excuses for neglecting to edit. But the most common excuse, by a mile, is time. "I just don't have time." I hear this constantly.

As it turns out, it's more costly *not* to edit because statistics consistently demonstrate that it costs more time to correct and/or clarify poorly written communication than it does to edit it effectively in the first place. For example, a business with 100 employees spends an average of 17 hours per week clarifying communication. This amounts to an annual loss of $528,443. Four hundred surveyed corporations estimated that poor communications (read: those that have not been effectively edited) cost the average organization $62.4 million per year in lost productivity.

I once coached a client on improved written communication. She was a program administrator at a large, high-revenue law firm. The quality of her communications was paramount to her success, and her digital communications were not hitting the mark. In addition to often containing what others viewed as a snarky or defensive tone, her emails and reports were often fraught with grammatical errors, punctuation errors, and typos. This is especially unacceptable in a field where even a misplaced comma can result in the misreading of a text that can cost a company millions of dollars. She sought me out because the situation had gotten so dire that her boss had placed her on final warning—she had to improve her communication or she was going to be fired. When she and I first sat down to discuss her situation, she must have given the excuse about time a dozen times in a dozen different ways. The law firm, she said, was fast-paced and high-stress, and people expected immediate answers. She simply did not have time to edit her communications. I asked her if she could commit to just one week of editing her communications before sending them. She said she could. I checked in with her by email after one week and she admitted to being shocked at what a difference she already saw. She had followed through on her promise and edited all her communications—even the short ones, including IMs. She noticed that she already felt better about what she was sending, and, more importantly, she had not had to take time to clarify, fix, or explain something after she had sent it. We agreed that she would try it for two more weeks. At our next meeting, which was in person, she had been editing her communications for three weeks. She was so excited about the difference that she was exuberant. She showed me an email from her boss in which he complimented her (something she said he had never done before) on the improved quality of her communications. And mind you, by this point, I had not even coached her on improved writing yet—all we had done was agree that she would edit what she had written.

About five months later, I received a beautiful goodie basket and card from her, thanking me. She had continued with all the new strategies she learned—editing arguably being the most important one. Her job had gotten so much better; not only was she no longer in danger of being fired, but she had also received a title promotion and raise. And she found herself coaching her peers on the strategies we had discussed. In the card, she said, "When we first met, I will admit I didn't believe you when you told me that editing would save me time.

I thought there was no way that could be true. But you were right, and I'm so glad I opened my mind to a new approach. Thank you!"

Another common excuse I hear for neglecting to edit is "I'm not an editor." That may be true, but you're likely not a professional writer either and you're doing that every day. Writing is a skill, and it can be practiced and honed; editing is a critical component of that practice. You may never know the ins and outs of comma use. That's okay. Commas are tough. I once took a two-day workshop on comma usage. Yep, two whole days on nothing but commas. I thought it was great fun, but you know what they say: one person's fun … At any rate, my point is that I understand that you may not have advanced-level grammatical knowledge. However, my focus here is on editing to correct the things you can, and I can assure you that, regardless of grammatical knowledge, you will find mistakes that you know how to correct. And even that will go a long way. This leads me to some specific strategies for editing your written work.

First, consider your first draft just that—a draft. Never (ever!) consider your first draft of anything final. Regardless of length, complexity, or even recipient, always edit your work before calling it final. My suggestion is to step away from the draft for a few minutes—again, yes, even if it's brief. This will allow you to return to it with fresh eyes. It works.

Second, embrace the notion that editing is much more than proofreading. Proofreading is looking for typos. But editing is looking for any issues that will detract from the clarity, conciseness, correctness, or completeness of your communication. Yes, you must edit for typos, but also for grammatical issues, missing or incorrect punctuation, confusing or superfluous verbiage, and tone. At a minimum, you should edit every digital communication for the following:

Grammar
Are you using correct grammar throughout to ensure understanding?

Punctuation
The proper use of commas and other punctuation makes your communication more readable and accurate.

Typos
Have you re-read your message to eliminate typos that can lead to misunderstandings and/or impact your credibility?

Clarity
See Chapter 3 for specifics on how to ensure clarity.

Problematic verbiage
Have you used any confusing language?

Have you used any superfluous verbiage?

Is there anything you can cut to make your message more concise while still being clear?

Have you said anything that could be misinterpreted or considered offensive?

Have you offered unsolicited opinions?

Missing information

What have you not said that may confuse the recipient(s)?
What have you said that needs evidence or support that you have not provided?

Tone

See Chapter 5 on tone and edit your communications to ensure the most positive tone possible.

Audience

Who will read this?
What do they already know?
What do they critically need to know?
What can or should you omit because it's not relevant to them?
What might you need to say differently given whom you're talking to?

Succinctness

Remember that recipients are not typically enthusiastic about reading someone else's stream of consciousness. So, edit to be sure you're succinct. There is one potential caveat to this suggestion. You can actually be too succinct. My #1 tip for avoiding that is never to say "sure." It's not uncommon for many people nowadays to respond to various requests and inquiries with the one-word response: sure. This often leaves the recipient with feelings of ambiguity—are you okay with this or not? I recommend choosing slightly less economy in this instance. You can avoid the need for relational repair by adding only two more words and replying, "It's my pleasure."

"Often people tend to feel that giving all the detail in an email is the way to make sure that they have covered the bases and provided clarity. Instead, the long-winded email does not get read or is skimmed and ends up confusing an issue (or being totally ignored). If you need to write more than a few bullets it may be best to have a quick meeting where two-way dialogue is present."

~ MaryBeth Costello, VP Talent, Learning & Corporate HR, Encore Global

My third strategy for editing is to read aloud. I covered this in Chapter 5, but it bears repeating here. When you read to yourself, you tend to read what you meant to write rather than what you actually wrote. You have a much greater likelihood of catching errors when you read aloud because you will read what's *actually* on the page, not what you *think* is on the page.

Fourth, get help. Even the strongest writers use trusted peers to review their communications. I do realize that this strategy takes even more time, so I am not suggesting you get a second pair of eyes on everything you write. But for particular occasions, such as an especially important document or recipient, I recommend asking someone you trust to review it. And encourage them to hold nothing back in their review. You will not only improve your communication, but you may also learn something new!

Finally, if you do not consider yourself a particularly strong writer, expand that knowledge. Unlike, say, learning a musical instrument or a new hobby, writing is something most people do every single day. There is no downside to expanding your vocabulary and your knowledge of grammar and punctuation.

Author Patricia Fuller is quoted as saying, "Writing without revising is the literary equivalent of waltzing gaily out of the house in your underwear." Make sure your communications are fully dressed. No one wants to see the sloppy underwear of bad writing.

Chapter 8

MISTAKE #8: THINKING YOU'RE TOO BUSY TO RESPOND TO OR FOLLOW UP WITH PEOPLE

Not too long ago, I was having lunch with a friend. We were both lamenting how busy we were until she stopped mid-sentence and said to me, "You know, let's not get into a busy-off with each other. What do you say we talk about something more positive?" I told her I thought that sounded great. And she was right—all most of us do these days is complain about how busy we are. It seems each of us thinks we're busier than everyone else—but if everyone thinks that, who's right? The truth is that we're all much too busy these days; it seems to be the state of human affairs.

What this tends to lead to, in terms of our digital communication, is a plethora of unanswered emails and a lack of follow-through. We scan our ever-growing list of to-dos, emails, IMs, and the like, and we determine which ones are critical while the rest can wait. But the problem is that "it can wait" often becomes, "it fell totally off my radar."

> "The modes meant to make communication easier can now also muddy it. We can have conversations via IM/text/chat and then have similar conversations in meetings/emails/phone calls. I've learned that different medium preferences often lead to follow-up issues. I, personally, prefer texts/IMs for questions, informal communication, etc. but prefer all task-oriented follow-ups to occur via email. For me, my email then serves as a to-do list that I can tackle. However, I've had two recent conversations with co-workers in which their preference is the exact opposite—they get an IM and immediately hop to the task at hand or mark it down to follow up on later; they feel email slows down this process for them. No one here is right. But if I'm waiting for an email to nudge me on something and my colleague asked me three days ago via chat surrounded by a series of other conversations or questions, I'm likely going to drop the ball. We both need to work to actively follow up with one another, since our work styles are

just different and stretch to make sure that communication flows in a two-way manner. I cannot assume that what works for me works for you, so I need to listen to what my colleague needs and respond to that."

~ Emily Brager, COO, CFPD (Colorado Fund for People with Disabilities)

Imagine a meeting with a client in which the client asked you to get her some information and you said to her, "Sally, I'll be honest with you. I'm going to tell you that I'll look into that, but as soon as this meeting is over, I'm going to forget, and you'll never hear from me again unless you bug me about it at least three times." I'm guessing that wouldn't go over well with your client (or your boss). But this is pretty much what happens with most of our emails nowadays.

And I get it—we're all busy. We all juggle too much, and things drop off our radar. It happens to the best of us—myself included.

But this is not good for our brand.

One of the main issues with lack of follow-through is that we respond or follow up with others based on how *we* prioritize items. Of course, our priorities aren't always the same as others' priorities, hence the disconnect. But keep in mind that, to any person, their needs rank highest. So, when we don't follow up with people, they may infer that we don't care about them or their needs. And this can lead to a lack of opportunities.

Let me offer an example. When I was a solopreneur, I engaged in copious amounts of networking. I was always trying to build relationships with people to establish a network of trusted colleagues as well as potential clients. I also tried to network with people whom I could help in return—focusing often on other small-business owners. One day I had lunch with a gentleman I'll call Rod, whom I had met at a networking event. He owned his own promotional-materials business. During our lunch, he went out of his way to tell me that he knew three different people he was certain would be interested in my services. He offered to connect me with them multiple times, emphasizing that he felt confident they would be interested. As one does when building relationships, I wanted to reciprocate, so I told him I had a few people in mind for his business as well.

I reached out to my contacts, confirmed that they were interested in connecting with Rod, and I followed up the next day with virtual connections. Over the next several weeks, I never heard from Rod concerning any connections for me, even though I contacted him several times; however, I also found out that he had made connections with the contacts I had suggested to him!

About six months later, I got a text one day out of the blue from Rod. It said, "Hey, Ali, this is Rod. I'm with a new promotional-materials company now. Let me know what needs you have for promotional items!" I was admittedly shocked that he had the courage to contact me given his lack of follow-through months earlier. He did not earn my business or any new referrals.

It may be easy to hear this story and think it's a one-off, or perhaps you think I'm being too hard on Rod. But I've shared it with a few trusted friends and colleagues, and they seem to support my stance that Rod's lack of follow-through several months back was unacceptable if he was looking to build a business relationship, and therefore, he didn't do much to earn my business nor any referrals to his.

I tell this story not to throw poor Rod under the bus, but to make the point that when we neglect to follow through with people—whether it's answering an email or following through on a commitment—it has the possibility of impacting how they perceive us and whether they are likely to champion us. We may lose their respect, we may miss out on internal opportunities, and we may lose clients.

But don't just take my word for it. Let's look at the research.

In an *Inc.* article, Eric Holtzclaw notes that lack of responsiveness can cost you, your employees or colleagues, and your company money. Similarly, in their landmark book, *The Leadership Challenge*, Jim Kouzes and Barry Posner call on their forty-plus years of research on leadership to note that integrity is the single-most "admired and sought-after" trait in leaders. When you do not exhibit follow-through—whether it's following through on your commitments or being responsive to your colleagues—you risk damaging your credibility.

In communication, behaviors fall into one of three categories: confirming, rejecting, or disconfirming. Confirming behaviors are behaviors that make the other person feel respected and valued—or at least heard. Confirming behaviors say, "The human in me recognizes the human in you." These are things like agreement, praise, and, yes, follow-through. Rejecting behaviors are behaviors like arguing, contradicting, complaining, insulting, and gossiping. Broadly speaking, they're messages of contempt. Disconfirming behaviors are, by far, the most damaging kinds of behaviors. They are behaviors that say to the other person, "I don't even care enough about you to respond," "You don't exist to me," or "You aren't valued." Disconfirming messages are far worse on a person's psyche and far more damaging to a relationship than even rejecting behaviors.

So, how does all of this translate to follow-through in our digital communication? Perhaps it's obvious by now, but the answer is that neglecting to follow through with someone is, simply put, a disconfirming behavior. It is the type of behavior that has the highest likelihood of doing the most damage to your professional relationship, the other person's view of you, and (as mentioned earlier) your potential opportunities.

People don't know your intentions. When you procrastinate responding to others (let's face it, often to the point of failing to respond), your colleagues cannot see your intention to respond "soon." All they see is that they still haven't heard from you.

Put yourself in others' shoes. Be honest. The last time you were waiting to hear back from someone but didn't, what negative stories did you tell yourself? About them? About why they aren't getting back to you? We've all done it. But do you really want to be on the receiving end of someone's hypothetical assumptions about why you aren't following up?

I acknowledged at the beginning of this chapter that we are all incredibly busy these days. And, unfortunately, I can't give you more time in the day. So, you must be wondering what solutions I can offer to help you with follow-through.

My first suggestion is to strategically manage your time. This suggestion probably comes as no surprise, and you've likely heard it a thousand times. Time management is key. Well, you've heard it so often because it's true. But do you make any real attempt to manage time? Do you have a system for prioritizing your tasks? When we feel overwhelmed by so much going on around us, it can be easy to throw up our hands (metaphorically or literally) and neglect to prioritize anything. But experts of all kinds note the many benefits of prioritizing tasks. Prioritizing helps decrease stress and anxiety, and it helps increase efficiency and productivity. Those are both pretty important outcomes. Lifehack.org also suggests that prioritizing helps you identify and earn more opportunities—due, in no small part, to the first two benefits coming together. If you're less stressed and more productive, you're more likely to have additional opportunities come your way.

There are myriad time-management and task-management tools and systems out there. I personally just use an old-school calendar/planner to write out my to-do lists each week. Regardless of what tool you use, my suggestion is to think critically about the criteria you use to prioritize your items. Think about your receivers, your colleagues, etc. rather than your preferences when you prioritize which items need immediate attention.

In Chapter 7, I discussed how important it is to consider your audience when writing any digital communication. Admittedly, this is a more complicated suggestion to follow when it comes to juggling multiple priorities. But it behooves us to try. Think about shifting your priorities to focus more on others—considering your audience instead of focusing on your own priorities.

We tend to prioritize the things we'd rather do, the things we're comfortable with, etc. Alice Boyes, in a 2018 *Harvard Business Review* article, noted that studies have found that people tend to prioritize low-importance or time-specific tasks over tasks that are more meaningful to them. For example, even though it may be more meaningful to you to finish a proposal for a prospective client, you tell yourself that the customer satisfaction survey from your mechanic is more important because it's easier to do, or that cleaning out your Spam box is critical so something you might need doesn't get inadvertently deleted.

Because of this, most resources on time management will urge you to prioritize more meaningful items over those that seem more urgent but are less important. For example, I found myself procrastinating the other day because I was nervous about something I had to write, so I told myself I simply **had** to order the picture frames to hang my wedding pictures in our hallway. Now, was that truly urgent? Of course not. But that's human nature—we need a "win," so we prioritize something easier to check off the to-do list.

My suggestion to manage your time is partly related to what Boyes talks about in her article, but it also relates to how you identify what IS meaningful to you. You must identify what matters to you, and what your deeper priorities are. Don't just consider what you prioritize in terms of tasks, but rather what you prioritize in terms of establishing your professional brand. When you think about it this way, you may find yourself prioritizing items differently.

So, as I said, most experts will urge you to prioritize items that truly matter over the less important short-term wins. And I concur. But my suggestion is to add an other-focused nuance to how we decide which items truly matter. Think big picture. Think about your professional reputation, about the brand you want to create for yourself. When you think about this, it may behoove you to prioritize items that are more important for someone else (at least for a specific purpose) than they are for you.

Am I suggesting that you should prioritize what is meaningful to someone else over what's meaningful to you? Definitely not. I am suggesting that you regard what's meaningful to your audience (client, colleague, etc.) as equally meaningful to you. For example, although it's faster and easier for me to book my travel for an upcoming vacation—which *is* meaningful to me—than it is to work on a request from my boss, I have to look at what is meaningful to me on a bigger-picture scale. Having my boss respect me and view me as dependable is incredibly important to me, so it behooves me to prioritize a task she has asked me to do.

The next suggestion to help you with follow through is to … well … follow through. Forgive the "Captain Obvious" nature of this suggestion, but sometimes we need reminders about the simple things. Perhaps the psychological and relationally based impacts of lack of follow-through that I've outlined in this chapter offer you the proverbial fire you needed in order to see them as more important, and now you're simply more likely to do it. If so, great!

If, like many others, any lack of follow-through on your part has more to do with a lack of time than a lack of desire, let me offer one additional suggestion: if you can't respond in full detail until a later date, get into the habit of responding immediately to acknowledge receipt of the person's communication. Let them know you have received their communication but that you won't be able to respond in detail until later. Here's the critical part of this suggestion—provide a specific date to hold yourself accountable, and calendar it so it stays on your radar!

When I managed a team at a former position, some of my team members used to be amazed (and, admittedly, teased me a bit) about the fact that I purportedly "never" forgot anything. But it wasn't that I had some magical memory—I simply kept track of the people I needed to respond to. When I suggested a date by which I would respond, I made sure I gave myself a realistic amount of time to look into the item and get back to them. Then I put it on my calendar to ensure it got done. Not magic—just a concerted effort to let my team know their needs were important to me.

And that's what following up does—it sends a message of importance. **We so often forget that effective communicators are those who make other people feel heard, supported, and important.**

Keep that in mind next time you think you don't have time to respond to someone, or that you'll "get to it later." How do you ensure that you are considered a strong communicator? You care less about your own time and more about ensuring that your colleague feels that her or his needs are important to you.

As a quick aside, but related to my last point, it is also incredibly helpful when you send something to someone else to let them know how urgently (or not) *you* need a response. Again, it shows a level of care and concern for their time to communicate whether you need a quick turnaround or whether something can wait until a particular date.

All these suggestions are in service of crafting your brand as a strong communicator. By now you're no doubt seeing a common thread among these chapters that a good portion of being a strong communicator has as much to do with how you treat others as the actual words you type or say. Do you remember the Golden Rule? Do unto others as you would have them do unto you. It's a good start, but it suggests that we begin with the assumption that others want to be treated the same way we do. The personal-assessment tool DiSC suggests a rule I like better: treat others the way *they* wish to be treated. That's the best rule to keep in mind as you consider how you follow up and follow through with others in your life. Keep the needs of your reader in mind each time you craft a message; say what you think they need to know rather than what (or how) you feel like writing.

Chapter 9

MISTAKE #9: HANDLING CONFLICT VIA DIGITAL COMMUNICATION

I n 2017, *Entrepreneur Magazine* published an article with a title that beautifully sums up the message of this chapter: "Using Email to Resolve Conflicts Is a Reliable Way of Making Everything Worse."

We live in an increasingly virtual society. It is so easy to fall back on using digital communication to accomplish everything. I'll fully admit that, if given the choice between calling or chatting with a customer service representative, I'll choose chat first unless I think I can't get my question answered that way (or it's been proven to me). There are many occasions in which the easier route is to use digital communication versus reaching out to someone via telephone or face-to-face. However tempting ease of use may be, using digital communication (email, IM, text, etc.) to handle conflict is just not a good idea.

I understand the inclination to handle conflict via email, text, or chat. Conflict is scary. When we talk to someone else about something that's bothering us, we make ourselves vulnerable. We may be afraid of how they will react. We may be afraid of damaging the relationship. But, if that is your fear (whether you acknowledge it consciously or not), why would you choose a route that increases the likelihood that you're making things worse? That seems to be a rather illogical choice.

Why not handle conflict the less scary way, you may ask? Well, let's start with the most pragmatic reason—my favorite kind. The bottom line is you are highly unlikely to resolve the issue this way. For all the reasons I have already covered in this book (see Chapter 5 on tone), we know that digital communication is, at best, an unreliable method for communicating your thoughts and emotions in a clear, reliable manner that lands in the most positive way for your recipient. At worst—and let's face it, "worst" is how it plays out a significant portion of the time—you risk truly making things worse because the person infers the worst possible tone, intention, and meaning from your words because they can't hear your tone or see your nonverbals.

Studies show that not only does email typically fail at helping address conflict proactively, but also, more often, it escalates it. This is, of course, due to the absence of critical nonverbal cues, such as facial expression, tone, and eye contact, between you and the recipient. These nonverbals are so important to help fill in the gaps between your words and your emotions that, without them, you are highly likely to create a misunderstanding of your written word, leading to the potential of escalating the conflict.

If your goal was to escalate the conflict, you likely wouldn't have bothered to send an email addressing it to begin with. We typically reach out to someone else to handle a conflict because we are bothered by something and wish to see it come to a resolution. So, if that's your goal, why would you take even the smallest risk that you will not only NOT solve it, but you might escalate it? I suppose I have to grant that if you truly don't care whether you damage the relationship, then email away. But remember that bridges can rarely, if ever, be unburned. I am not proud to admit that even I have found this out the hard way. But I learned my lesson, and my hope is that this chapter will serve as your lesson so that you forgo learning it the hard way as I did.

Maybe you don't think you tend to handle conflict digitally, so this chapter isn't relevant to you. If that's true, good for you! But…are you sure? Have you ever said something to someone in an email, IM, or text that you would never say to their face? (If you said "no" to this, I want to challenge you to be more self-reflexive; most people have to honestly say "yes" to this question.) People tend to think "handling conflict by digital communication" means that they had a fight or disagreement with someone else by email, text, or IM. But I'm referring to saying anything via digital communication that involves a topic that may be contentious in any way—that includes anything overly complex, since a lack of understanding may lead to contentious feelings.

You may be either encouraged or dismayed (depending on your disposition, I suppose) to hear that some experts suggest there are circumstances in which it is acceptable to handle difficult conversations via digital communication. Some notable examples of this include the following:

To request a face-to-face, visual virtual call, or phone call to discuss the matter.

This is a great way to use digital communication with regard to handling a conflict situation. It is acceptable to reach out to the other concerned party(ies) to request a face-to-face or virtual meeting to discuss the matter. In this situation, it is imperative to resist any temptation to discuss the actual conflict in this communication. Keep your communication relegated to the request itself.

For example, **don't** write:

> *Jamie, clearly, we are at an impasse about the proposal to the board. I don't think you understand what we need to do. We need to get together to discuss this. How about this Tuesday at 3?*

Instead, write something like this:

> *Jamie, I'd love to discuss our collaboration on the board proposal. How about this Tuesday at 3:00 via Zoom?*

Keep it short, sweet, and as objective as possible. Eliminate all references to feelings, emotions, judgments of others' actions, etc.

When There Needs to Be a Record of the Conversation

Although I have seen experts assert it's acceptable to handle conflict in these cases, I still do not recommend it. Instead, use the previous suggestion to reach out with a request to discuss the matter. Then, after said discussion has taken place, you may follow up with an email to confirm what was discussed and agreed upon.

For example:

Jamie,

Thanks so much for meeting with me yesterday to discuss the board proposal; I appreciate your time. As promised, I'm following up with a quick email to confirm what we agreed upon:

You will complete the proposal based on the feedback we talked through yesterday.

You will send me the proposal by COB this Friday for any edits.

Once we are both comfortable with the draft, we will send it to Connie for review by next Friday.

Let me know if I've inadvertently omitted anything we agreed on yesterday.

Best,
Ali

When Dealing with Conflicts Where the Emotion Is Relatively Low

I concur with this suggestion, so long as you feel highly confident in your assessment of low emotion. For example, you might use digital communication when you are trying to agree on a date for a team meeting. This example illustrates the truly low-emotion nature that the "conflict" at hand should have to use digital communication to discuss it.

Only as a Last Resort When Time Is of the Essence

Somewhat begrudgingly I admit that there may be situations when time is of the essence and, thus, engaging in conflict digitally is necessary. For example, I recently needed to discuss a potentially challenging situation with a client, and time was short since we needed to discuss it before an upcoming meeting with others. I had emailed and called her several times but received no response. Thus, I did send my thoughts digitally.

In these situations, it is important to ensure that it truly is a last resort. And if you must handle something digitally, there are some suggestions for doing so as effectively as possible:

Do everything you can to communicate positive intent. Recall the earlier chapter on tone. It is notoriously difficult to adequately convey your actual feelings, emotions, and intent digitally; nonetheless, when you absolutely have to use digital communication to discuss a potentially challenging situation, it behooves you to try. In such cases, you may try approaches such as one of the following:

> *I would like to discuss our project before our meeting this Friday. I want to convey my sincere optimism for this collaboration; I know we can accomplish great things. So, let's please get together as soon as possible to discuss how we can ensure a successful project.*

Or

> *It has been brought to my attention that you shared a concern with Frances about my plan. I'd love to discuss this. I recognize it can be difficult to convey positive intent by email, so I want to be clear that I am not upset in any way. I simply want to suggest that we have a conversation to determine how you and I can best collaborate on this.*

If these two examples seem a bit verbose, that's purposeful. When it comes to handling challenging situations, I suggest that you cannot be too careful about stating positive intent. You'll notice in the second example I even named the difficulty of conveying positivity via email. The more you can call attention to the difficulty of the medium and your genuine positive intent, the better.

Never, ever send your email without stepping away from it first. Ideally, you should even write your email twice. *Harvard Business Review* suggests you write it first for content, then step away from it. When you come back to it, re-read it, imagining the potential impact of every single phrase on the recipient(s). Now, with that impact in mind, re-write the message, taking great care to address the potential impact of various phrases. For example, you might have originally written, "The report the team wrote contains numerous errors." Upon rewriting it, you might add, "I am smiling as I imagine the enthusiasm and hard work the team put into this report. I believe that will be more efficiently conveyed once we can ensure it is free from errors." In this way, you can "help control others' interpretation" of your written words.

Always step away from any email (conflict topic or not) and re-read it to ensure it does the best possible job of conveying what you mean it to convey. And when it comes to challenging topics, my suggestion is that the more challenging the topic, the more time you should allow between the original writing of the message and sending it—step away for longer and re-read it more times.

Never editorialize about the other person's actions, intent, etc. The only person's intent we can ever be 100 percent certain of is our own (and for less-self-aware people, even that isn't always possible). So, when using digital communication to discuss challenging situations, avoid any subjective statements about the intent behind someone else's actions, words, etc.

For example, **don't** write:

> *You obviously didn't spend much time on this report.*

or

> *It's clear you and I aren't on the same page.*

You cannot know with 100 percent certainty that either of those statements—or any other statement of the same ilk—is true. So, leave them out. Subjective opinions do nothing but add fuel to the potential conflict fire.

Even if you think you're giving the other person the benefit of the doubt (for example, "You obviously didn't mean to hurt my feelings …"), leave out any subjective opinion. Again, you don't know if this is true. Perhaps the person did mean to hurt your feelings; now all you've done is once again stoke a potential disagreement.

The bottom line is that any email, text, or IM dealing with a potentially challenging or conflictual topic should be 100 percent objective. State facts and leave the rest out.

Avoid sarcasm and humor. When using digital communication to talk about something difficult, there is typically little room for sarcasm or humor because they can be so easily misinterpreted (think about how many jokes fall flat if recipients aren't in the right mindset to hear them.) How could you possibly know what mindset your recipient will be in when they read your communication? You can't control when they read it, what is going on around them when they do, what kind of day they're having, etc. And even if you *could* control those things, that is still no guarantee they share your mindset. Therefore, control what you can, which is your message. Keep it simple, concise, on-point, and free from statements that can be easily misinterpreted.

Speaking of things that can be easily misinterpreted, I often get asked how I feel about people using emojis and text language (LOL, IMO, etc.). I'm a modern human, so I use them as often as anyone in everyday digital communications. However, they do fall under the category of being easily misinterpreted. Therefore, I do not recommend using emojis or text-speak when communicating digitally about a challenging subject. Remember that your goal is as much clarity and objectivity as possible. Emojis and text-speak typically lessen clarity. You might be thinking, "What about a smiley face? How could someone misinterpret a smiley face?" Well … I happen to have just such an example.

A friend of mine once sent an email to a colleague to follow up on a conversation they had had about a project they were working on that wasn't going well. The way she put it to me, the conversation was tense, and they both seemed unsure of what to do next, so they just left issues hanging rather awkwardly. She followed up with this email:

Hey Arlene,

Sorry about earlier. I hope you don't think I'm upset with you. I was simply trying to make it clear that I really care about this project, and I'm sure you do, too. 😊 *Let's chat again next week. I'm sure we can work something out.*

Seems like a fairly innocuous email, right? That's what my friend thought. The next week, she arrived at work to find an icy reception from Arlene. She couldn't figure out what the problem was, so she asked Arlene in person if everything was okay. Arlene said to her, "I DO care about this project, you know." My friend was taken aback. Arlene's comment suggested that she thought my friend assumed Arlene did not care about the project when her email clearly stated otherwise. But Arlene had taken the winky face as sarcasm—as in, "Suuure you care about this project."

This example just goes to show a point I feel I cannot over-state: you simply never know when relational history, personal experience, and subjective perception will combine to ensure a wildly different interpretation of the written word—or emoji—than you had intended.

So, keep it simple: when it comes to conflict via digital com-munication, stick to words, and keep them as objective and clear as possible.

I've had people ask me some version of the question, "But what if I receive an email from someone else that is mean, hos-tile, passive-aggressive, etc.?" In other words, if someone else has chosen to handle conflict digitally with *you*, what recourse do you have? In previous chapters, I've asserted that the onus is always on us as communicators to make the most efficacious choice—for the situation, the relationship, our communicative goals, etc. This is no different.

Think about that scenario from the perspective of face-to-face communication. If someone says something mean, hostile, or passive-aggressive to your face, do you have a choice about how to respond? Of course, you do. You have the right to *feel* whatever emotional response occurs naturally as the result of such a comment; however, the mark of emotional intelligence is knowing what to DO with those feelings. Emotionally intelligent individuals choose productive responses—responses that reflect long-term thinking and honor the relationship over a fleeting emotional response. Digital communication should be no different. I'll assert it should be even easier to choose a more productive response to a negative email, IM, or text because there is no reason whatsoever you have to respond right away. Take the time, step back from it, and make the most productive choice possible.

Trust me, you'll always be glad you did. No one in the history of time has EVER looked back and said, "Geez, I really wish I had sent an angry, poorly worded email to that person."

Chapter 10

LOOKING THROUGH THE EI LENS

n this book, I've explored mistakes you may be making when you communicate digitally (Zoom/Teams, email, IM, text) that could be holding you back. When I say these mistakes are holding you back, I mean personally and professionally. Perhaps they're even holding you back from a self-fulfillment perspective; it's been my experience that, however subconsciously, we often know when we aren't meeting our full potential.

Let's review the mistakes:

- Thinking Your Industry Knowledge is the Only Thing That Matters
- Thinking That the Onus is on the Other Person to Figure Out What You Mean When Your Communication is Unclear or Poorly Written
- Thinking IM Communication Doesn't Count
- Thinking Your Tone Doesn't Matter Because People Know You Mean Well
- Thinking It's OK That You're Not Mentally Present in a Zoom Meeting Because You're Good at Multi-tasking
- Thinking You Don't Have Time to Edit and Thinking Short Communications Don't Need to Be Edited
- Thinking You're Too Busy to Respond to or Follow Up with People
- Handling Conflict via Digital Communication

In each chapter, I offered tips and tactics for mitigating or altogether avoiding these mistakes. In this chapter, I am suggesting a more overarching strategy that applies to all digital-communication issues. Perhaps you've thought of some additional digital-communication mistakes I haven't covered in this book? If so, kudos to you for doing so. The information I'll share in this chapter will help guide you toward mitigating any communication issues.

The strategy in this chapter is framed as a lens through which you should view every **single** digital communication you craft: instant messages, texts, emails, and even social media posts. Imagine putting on a pair of glasses that will enable you to see each digital communication you send through this helpful lens; in fact, let's take it even further. I want you to imagine you can't see to type *without* these glasses; you *have to* wear them.

I call it the EI Lens. But this is not your mom's EI (in other words, emotional intelligence); this stands for Empathy and Inquiry. In this context, I'm referring to empathy and inquiry as strategic choices; they are skills you can proactively choose to practice and hone.

First, practice **empathy** for others in your digital communications. You may or may not naturally be a particularly empathetic person. And if you're not, that's OK. What I'm suggesting here is that you use the practice of empathy as a skill; that is, proactively make the choice to consider the impact of your communicative message on the other person. How might it land with them? What might the impact be? How might they receive it, hear it, etc.? Will they understand it as written?

This consideration of the impact of your message includes whether the message makes sense, whether it's timely, whether it's too wordy or abrupt, and what the overall tone is. You must consider the impact of your communication on the other person, not necessarily because it's the right thing to do—although it is—but more so because it's the right strategic choice to improve YOUR communication.

Think about this: How many times have you written what you felt like saying instead of what your recipient needed to know? When you do this, you fail to accomplish your communicative goals.

Let's look at this from a purely scientific perspective in terms of how our brains are wired. You may recall that in Chapter 3, I explained that you can think of your brain as comprised of trillions of tiny little storage cubbies and that each thing you've ever learned is stored in one of those cubbies. But because the world is full of too many stimuli for our brain to attend to all of it, the brain prioritizes what to pay attention to. And prior experience with incoming data ensures that our brain will use a strong signal to process that stimulus.

To put this into simple terms, when you communicate with other people, if you can't somehow connect what you're saying to something that already exists in their heads, your message will NOT land. It may create confusion, and the recipients will likely ignore it and/or forget it.

This means it is always—100 percent of the time, regardless of your medium (text, IM, email, etc.)—your responsibility as the communicator to provide clarity and context to create pathways between what you're saying and what exists in one of the little cubbies in your recipient's head.

A former boss of mine some years ago frequently neglected to provide clarity **or** context in her communications. I sometimes legitimately believed she thought I was capable of reading her mind. She would email me things like, "Did you get to that yet?" I had a dozen tasks on deck that day, several dozen per week, so...to what did "that" refer? It was unclear.

Or I would IM her and ask something like, "Do you want me to edit the State-of-the-Campus report for you now or after you include the visuals?" to which she would respond with simply "Yes." Or she would respond with something completely unrelated like, "I think Terri wants to be included in the meeting tomorrow."

Sometimes, examples like these are funny, but not usually until later. In the moment, they're usually frustrating, they waste time, and they risk damaging the sender's credibility.

Imagine I'm your manager, and consider the following IM exchange:

You say: *I think I found something.*

I think: *OK … a hair in your food? Bigfoot? The meaning of life? What?*

Instead, respect my time by taking a bit more of your own, and say:

"In the meeting about the Jupiter project we had yesterday, you asked me if I could find some code to unblock us from moving forward. I think I found it."

When you're communicating with others, keep in mind that there is no way to read your mind. Empathy in this context means you must choose to consider your reader EACH time you write. You must take care to ensure that your message connects with them—that is, you proactively consider how to craft a message that will make sense to them and matter to them. Otherwise, their brains will just filter your words out as more of the digital noise we're all bombarded with every day.

The second part of the EI equation is **inquiry**. In the previous section, I suggested that you must write what the other person needs to know, not what you feel like saying (or think you have time to write). But how do you know what they need to know? The answer: you ask questions.

Again, I'm using this term strictly from a skills perspective. I'm not asking you to become a more curious person in general (though if you are, this skill may already be a bit more natural for you). What I mean is that you should learn to constantly ask questions about your digital communications, including written messages and how you show up in virtual meetings.

Ask questions about your message before you send it, questions like:

What is the purpose of this piece of communication?

If you don't know what you're trying to achieve with a particular communication, how can you expect your recipient(s) to? To craft clear, concise communication, it's imperative that you are clear on exactly what you're trying to accomplish with that message. Often, we think we are writing something to convey pertinent information or to make a request or suggestion, but instead, we end up merely communicating our feelings about a topic.

A colleague of mine, whom I'll call Lawrence, shared a great example of this with me recently. He received this IM from a colleague of his (whom I'll name Morgan):

I'm worried about Rene's response to Judd's suggestion. What do you think?

This IM left Lawrence befuddled. What was Morgan asking of Lawrence? Did he want Lawrence to respond that he shared Morgan's concern? Did he want him to opine as to whether Rene's response was appropriate? To offer an opinion on Judd's suggestion? It was entirely unclear to Lawrence what Morgan was asking for.

This is a short but effective example to illustrate my point. Make sure that, before you waste someone else's time by sending a message with no clear point or directive, that you are sure of the goal of the message yourself.

What might be misinterpreted?

- About what I've said?
- About how I said it?
- About why I left certain information out?
- About why I'm off camera?
- About why I'm clearly doing something else while my colleague is talking?
- About why I haven't followed up with this person for X number of days (or weeks)?

What context or information have I not provided?

You can go back to the fundamentals here: who, what, when, where, how, and why. You don't have to address every one every time, but they're useful guides for considering what information may be pertinent that you've inadvertently left out. Ask yourself what the other person needs to know rather than what you feel like saying—or worse, what you have time to type.

It's especially important to inquire into what you haven't said because the *missing* information is most often the source of the lack of clarity—maybe even more so than what you *do* say.

For example, if you email me and say, "Hey, I took care of that project. We're all set," I'm going to have a lot of questions. Which project? Took care of it how, exactly? Who is "we"? And what does "all set" mean to you? (We may have different ideas of what it means to be "all set.") Provide as much information as you can, taking care to do so clearly and concisely.

When you lead from a place of inquiry (and empathy), you learn to start writing from your recipients' points of view instead of yours and thus ask yourself questions about what is clear and unclear in each communication.

Not only should you ask yourself questions about your own communication to amp up clarity and context, but you can also use inquiry to ask yourself questions about others' communications. When you receive communicative messages from others that are unclear, incomplete, hurtful, or otherwise bothersome, you can ask questions like:

- What might I be misinterpreting?
- Is it possible they meant something different than how I'm taking it? (The answer to this question is almost always "yes.")
- What could I ask to clarify something before jumping to conclusions?

- What could I ask this person to connect with them better?
- What information do I need that they haven't provided?

Using inquiry in this manner will lead to improved communication between you and others (as well as improved relationships) because it will help you avoid assumptions about others' communication. And it will help you, in turn, continue to ask more questions for clarification instead of proceeding with misinformation or missing information.

Remember that, as I explained in Chapter 6, attention is selective. Use empathy and inquiry each time you communicate, regardless of the context, to ensure that your messages are clear and succinct. Not because your recipients have a short attention span, but because your communication must connect to what they know and understand for their brains to **selectively** attend to it.

There's a bonus to employing the EI Lens. In the first chapter, I asked you to consider whether you may be a digital polluter. If you use empathy and inquiry to craft all your communications, not only will you avoid making the communication mistakes discussed in this book, but you will also create communications that command people's attention, which will increase the likelihood that your messages are understood, addressed, and appreciated. All of this will solidify your brand. And remember (again, harkening back to Chapter 1) that your communication IS your brand. Like it or not and intentional or not, you DO have a brand. And your communication is a massive part of that brand in the eyes of your contacts.

Don't use digital communication as an excuse to not bring your BEST self. Show up the same way virtually as you would in person. If anything, pay more attention to your digital communications. The more you can refrain from contributing to the digital clutter (by taking the extra minute now to proofread, ensure clarity, etc.) the more people will count on you as a partner. The more credibly you'll be perceived. The more you will rise to the top.

Years ago, I attended a transformative retreat focused on being good to ourselves and others. I learned a phrase there that has stuck with me ever since: **This Moment Matters.** What does that phrase call to mind for you? Sit with that for a moment if you will.

I found it to be powerful for two reasons. First, because the intent behind the phrase is to illustrate that every time we think something doesn't matter…well…it does. The phrase is applicable in this context; for example, every time we fire off a terse email that could have been worded more collaboratively and tell ourselves that it doesn't matter for any number of reasons (I don't have time, they'll understand I'm in a hurry, they were rude to me last time, etc.) simply put, we are wrong. It **does** matter. Every one of those matters to the other person.

It's also powerful for another reason: this phrase, which sounds rather esoteric, is scientifically accurate. How so? You may recall that in Chapter 3, I explained that when we learn something, we create a literal pathway in the brain—a physical neural pathway. And behavior chosen over and over is learned behavior. Thus, every time you decide to take some particular course of action, you are re-engaging with that pathway, making it deeper. If you decide to take a **new** course of action, you must choose to take that same new course of action again and again—

each moment it comes up—to make the new pathway as deep as the original one. So, each time you choose the new (if you'll grant it, better) pathway, you deepen that path, making it easier to take the next time. All that is to say, this moment **does** matter.

To bring this back full circle to your communications, every single time you choose to engage in the best practices outlined in this book, you deepen that neural pathway. And every single time you choose to ensure a positive tone, be fully present in a Zoom meeting, or take time to edit a communication (even a short one!), you are deepening that new neural pathway, making it more likely each time that you will choose that route again the next time.

I find it so encouraging and affirming to know that making the proactive choice to enhance our brand via our communication tactics is just that—a **choice**. You need not be beholden to the assumption, "This is just the way I am." Ultimately, communication isn't about who you are; it's about what you say and what you do. And each time you choose to engage in digital communication using the EI lens, you will make it less likely that you make one of the mistakes discussed in this book. And each time you make that choice, it becomes easier to make it again the next time.

Remember the adage, "Dress for the job you want, not the job you have"? I think the same idea applies here. Choose digital-communication practices that reflect the person you want others to see you as—the person you know you can be. Where will you begin?

LET'S CONTINUE
THIS JOURNEY

I t is my passion in life to help others craft exemplary communication skills because they create stronger relationships with everyone in our lives. If you would like to continue this journey, there are several ways to do that.

- Follow me (Ali Atkison) on LinkedIn.
- Take my Great Courses course, The Brain-based Guide to Communicating Better, at www.thegreatcourses.com or streaming on Wondrium (available on Roku).
- Connect with me through HRD–A Leadership Development Company if you're interested in having your

leadership team participate in my Brain-based Leadership workshop series.

- If you've enjoyed this book, please review it and share your favorite story, strategy, or other takeaway.

My last request is that you lead your life with my favorite piece of advice from Ted Lasso: Be curious, not judgmental.

Thank you for creating a space for this book in your life. I hope it serves you well.

Most sincerely,

Ali Atkison

ABOUT THE AUTHOR

D r. Ali Atkison is a highly regarded keynote speaker and facilitator who has educated and inspired audiences of all sizes for more than two decades. With a Ph.D. in Human Communication Studies and more than twenty years in higher education, Ali is widely considered one of the foremost authorities on how the adult brain learns. Ali has a wealth of experience in professional speaking, learning and development, facilitation, leadership, and coaching. She uses her experience with the power of communication and science to deliver results that marry the complex interplay between human communication choices and the organization's values and mission. Ali has published articles in *ATD Magazine*, UPCEA's *Unbound*, and *The Chronicle of Higher Education*. She has appeared on numerous podcasts including Geeks, Geezers, and Googlization and LinkedIn Live with Dr. Laura Sicola. She is the professor and creator of self-paced digital courses for Wondrium and Audible on brain-based tactics for communication, written communications, and consulting. And she has conducted keynotes and workshops on brain-based communication skills for organizations such as Marsh McLennan, Pinnacol Assurance, the Denver Art Museum, Advisa Group, Denver Public Library, National Association for Graduate Admissions Professionals, the Montana University System, the Institute for Adult Learning in Singapore, and more.

Ali works with a phenomenal team at HRD A Leadership Development Company, where she serves clients all over the world by fostering exemplary leadership and communication skills.

Ali currently resides in Indianapolis, Indiana with her husband, Adam; their dog, Sofia; and Adam's three boys, Owen, Griffin, and Camden, who don't live with them but are ever-present in their hearts.

ENDNOTES

Chapter 1

Beute, Ethan and Stephen Pacinelli. *Human-Centered Communication*. New York: Fast Company Press, 2021.

Chapter 2

Hoover, Brad. "Good Grammar Should Be Everyone's Business," *Harvard Business Review*, March 4, 2013, https://hbr.org/2013/03/good-grammar-should-be-everyon.

Kaufman, Josh. *The First 20 Hours: How to Learn Anything… Fast*. New York: Penguin, 2013.

Hunt, James and Joseph Weintraub. *The Coaching Manager: Developing Top Talent in Business*. Los Angeles: Sage, 2017.

Chapter 3

Queensland Brain Institute. *Action Potentials and Synapses.* Queensland, Australia, https://qbi.uq.edu.au/brain-basics/ brain/brain-physiology/action-potentials-and-synapses#:~: text=Synapse%20%E2%80%93%20The%20junction%20 between%20the,which%20the%20two%20neurons%20 communicate.

Zull, James. *The Art of Changing the Brain: Enriching the Practice of Teaching by Exploring the Biology of Learning.* New York: Routledge. 2002.

Chapter 4

Liu, Alicia. "Death by a Thousand Pings: The Hidden Side of Using Slack," *Medium*, March 20, 2018, https://medium. com/counter-intuition/the-hidden-side-of-using-slack-2443d9b66f8a.

Molla, Rani. "The Productivity Pit: How Slack is Ruining Work," *Vox*, May 1, 2019, https://www.vox.com/ recode/2019/5/1/18511575/productivity-slack-google-microsoft-facebook.

Thompson, Jeff. "Is Nonverbal Communication a Numbers Game?" *Psychology Today*, September 30, 2011, https://www.psychologytoday.com/us/blog/beyond-words/201109/is-nonverbal-communication-a-numbers-game.

Brown, Brene. *Dare to Lead.* New York: Random House. 2018.

Byron, Kris. "Carrying Too Heavy a Load? The Communication and Miscommunication of Emotion by Email." *Acad-*

emy of Management Review 33, no. 2. (April 2008). https://
journals.aom.org/doi/10.5465/amr.2008.31193163.

Jaffe, Eric. "Why It's So Hard to Detect Emotion in Emails
and Texts," *Fast Company*, October 9, 2014. https://www.
fastcompany.com/3036748/why-its-so-hard-to-detect-
emotion-in-emails-and-texts.

Chapter 6

Medina, John. *Brain Rules*. Seattle: Pear Press. 2014.

Dumont, Theron Q. *The Power of Concentration*. Reprint.
Deautschland: Jazzybee Verlag. 2015 (1918).

Ferguson, Sian. "One Minute of Meditation a Day is Good
Enough (Really)," *Healthyway*, (n.d.) https://www.
healthyway.com/content/one-minute-of-meditation-a-day-
is-good-enough-really/.

Chapter 7

Haden, Jeff. "How One Missing Comma Just Cost This Company $5 Million (But Did Make Its Employees $5 Million
Richer)," *Inc.*, February 12, 2018, https://www.inc.com/
jeff-haden/how-1-missing-comma-just-cost-this-company-5-
million-but-did-make-its-employees-5-million-richer.html.

Chapter 8

Holtzclaw, Eric. "The Importance of Responsiveness," *Inc.*,
April 13, 2015. https://www.inc.com/eric-holtzclaw/
the-importance-of-responsiveness.html.

Kouzes, James and Barry Posner. *The Leadership Challenge: How to Make Extraordinary Things Happen in Organizations.* Hoboken: Wiley & Sons. 2023.

Ho, Leon. "The Ultimate Guide to Prioritizing Your Work and Life," *LifeHack,* August 16, 2023. https://www.lifehack.org/810807/prioritizing-work-and-life#why-is-prioritizing-important.

Boyes, Alice. "How to Focus on What's Important, Not Just What's Urgent," *Harvard Business Review*, July 3, 2018. https://hbr.org/2018/07/how-to-focus-on-whats-important-not-just-whats-urgent.

Chapter 9

Friedman, Raymond and Steven Currall. "Conflict Escalation: Dispute-Exacerbating Elements of Email Communication." *Human Relations* 56, no. 11 (2003). 1325–1347.

Grenny, Joseph. "You Can Have Constructive Conflict Over Email," *Harvard Business Review*, March 24, 2015. https://hbr.org/2015/03/you-can-have-constructive-conflict-over-email.

A free ebook edition is available with the purchase of this book.

To claim your free ebook edition:

1. Visit MorganJamesBOGO.com
2. Sign your name CLEARLY in the space
3. Complete the form and submit a photo of the entire copyright page
4. You or your friend can download the ebook to your preferred device

Morgan James BOGO™

A **FREE** ebook edition is available for you or a friend with the purchase of this print book.

CLEARLY SIGN YOUR NAME ABOVE

Instructions to claim your free ebook edition:
1. Visit MorganJamesBOGO.com
2. Sign your name CLEARLY in the space above
3. Complete the form and submit a photo of this entire page
4. You or your friend can download the ebook to your preferred device

Print & Digital Together Forever.

Snap a photo

Free ebook

Read anywhere